# PRAIRIE FEAST

# Prairie Feast

*a writer's journey home for dinner.*

AMY JO EHMAN

www.coteaubooks.com

Edited by Roberta Coulter
Designed by Tania Craan

**Library and Archives Canada Cataloguing in Publication**

Ehman, Amy Jo, 1962-
      Prairie feast : a writer's journey home for dinner / Amy Jo Ehman.

Includes index.
ISBN 978-1-55050-413-2

      1. Ehman, Amy Jo, 1962-.  2. Cookery, Canadian--Prairie style.
3. Food habits--Prairie Provinces.  4. Local foods--Prairie Provinces.
I. Title.

TX715.6.E398 2010        641.59712        C2010-901019-1

10  9  8  7  6  5  4  3  2  1

2517 Victoria Avenue
Regina, Saskatchewan
Canada   S4P 0T2
www.coteaubooks.com

*Available in Canada from:*
Publishers Group Canada
9050 Shaughnessy Street
Vancouver, BC
Canada   V6P 6E5

Coteau Books gratefully acknowledges the financial support of its publishing program by: the Saskatchewan Arts Board, the Canada Council for the Arts, the Government of Canada through the Canada Book Fund, the Government of Saskatchewan through the Creative Economy Entrepreneurial Fund, the Association for the Export of Canadian Books and the City of Regina Arts Commission.

*To John, my dinner partner.*

# TABLE OF CONTENTS

# 1
# HATS OFF TO DINNER

## REDISCOVERING TASTE ONE BITE AT A TIME

- - - - - - - - - - - - - - - - - - - - - - - - - - - - - - - - -

THIS STORY BEGINS WITH A PIG and a little red hat. The pig is long gone, and delicious he was. The little red hat remains as a symbol of my first forays into the fresh and flavourful world of local foods.

Before my little pig, I wasn't fussy about the food I ate. I never thought about where it was raised or how it was grown or whether it saw the sky or felt the sun. I was raised on a farm, and even though we grew our own vegetables, picked berries and raised chickens, I learned early in life that most food comes from a supermarket, where the most important factors are convenience and price. By the time I had my own kitchen, I was as far removed from the source of my food as the next urban working gal sidling her grocery cart up to the till.

That little pig changed everything.

It began on one of those first promising days of spring. A day when you want to stand taller and smell deeper and your heart wants to leap like a new lamb. When sage hillsides are dotted with feathery crocuses, but down in the lake shards of ice still float here and there like pieces of broken china. A day when a warm south wind blows so furiously it feels as if the floodgates of spring have been thrown open in one mad, impetuous rush, winter be damned.

My husband John and I were visiting friends who had recently moved from Victoria to a small farm near Regina Beach. They were prairie folks who didn't much like the West Coast. Victoria was too damp and too crowded. Here on the farm, the sense of space was enormous and the air was weightless and dry. There was a small red barn, a corral made of worn grey fence posts and several wooden outbuildings, one of which had been turned into a woodworking shop. The pasture ran to the crest of the hill and down the steep slope to Last Mountain Lake.

After a long walk in the grassy hills, we sat down to dinner in the big farmhouse. It was here, around the dinner table, that our friend Art declared his intention to raise some pigs. Pigs, he said, would keep his children busy over the summer months. Since the kids were being home-schooled, the pigs would provide valuable lessons in science, mathematics, accounting, animal husbandry and a bit of physical education too, while adding to the family larder at the same time.

How wonderfully old-fashioned. It took me back to my childhood, when, for a few years, my dad raised pigs for our own dinner table. I loved those pigs. They were cute and friendly, and, for a short time before they grew up, we were permitted to play with them. And I was always aware that one day those pigs would be bacon and pork chops. Which I loved, too.

"If you're raising pigs," I said to Art, "raise one for us."

It was a spontaneous request made after much wine and goodwill. By morning, I had forgotten all about it. But Art hadn't. And later that year, long after the trees were bare and the tomatoes were ripening in the basement, he sent an email to tell us our pig had an appointment with a butcher block.

Suddenly remembering my rash request, and quite unsure what kind of damage a whole pig would do to our pocketbook, I dashed an email back to Art to inquire what I might expect to pay for our pig. But where I should have typed the word "pay," my brain crossed gears and told my fingers to type the word "buy" instead.

"What should I expect to buy for our pig?"

"That's a strange question," Art wrote back, "but now that you ask, perhaps a little red hat would be nice."

I went to a second-hand store and bought a little red hat. It was a knit hat for a toddler, with earflaps from which ran two long strings for tying under the chin. No matter that such a little hat would never fit on the head of a pig, it was the thought that counted – the thought of eating a pig that had rolled in the mud, played with children, basked in the sunshine and slept at night in a little red barn. It was the pig of my childhood, and I had the little red hat to prove it.

ONE OF MY FONDEST MEMORIES of growing up on the farm was the day we slaughtered the pigs. By now, the pigs were far too large for play-mates. They were big and ornery, and I was, I suspect, no older than six. I remember a frosty grey day in fall, a jacket-and-mittens day, long after the leaves had disappeared but before the snow fell. A day when the last long lines of geese passed overhead squawking and I would twist my head around to watch, wondering what took them so long to get up and go. We had already pulled the garden, plucked the chickens and put the storm windows on the house. We were ready for winter, with one final task: to dispatch the pigs.

Dad raised four pigs, just enough for our family and to give some to the folks who came out to help. Pig day was likely to attract a number of neighbours, including my bachelor uncles Paul and Bill who lived up the road in a big old farmhouse surrounded by well-tended orchards. Grandma and Grandpa Ehman came out from town, and so did my city cousins, who seemed to regard the farm in a way that a farm kid can't quite understand. To me, the farm was home; to them, it was an adventure vacation. To me, it was a place of work and productivity; to them, it was an amusement park. To me, it was full of boundaries; to them, it was as boundless as the virgin prairie. On one visit, my city cousin Richard got himself sprayed by a skunk, something I had managed to avoid through a whole childhood on the farm. They were boys, they were bigger and they were brave. But on pig day, they were about to learn a thing or two about the hazards of country life.

As for those pigs, Dad tells me he dispatched them with a shotgun, then quickly cut a vein in their necks to drain the blood. I don't remember that part. We children were ushered inside at that critical moment. This was, I am told, not because we might be traumatized by the finality of it all but because, as my dad says, a bullet *could* ricochet.

Yes, we were farm kids and quite aware even at that tender age that every hot dog and bologna sandwich was once an animal that grew up on a farm. We knew first-hand the origin of the saying "run around like a chicken with its head cut off," having chased down more than a few of those over the years. Dad was obviously more comfortable wielding an axe in front of his children than a gun.

Once the pigs had met their fate and were hanging eviscerated from a beam in the shop, we were allowed back outside. Their bodies were still warm and smelled of clean raw meat. A day later, Dad carved them into their deconstructed pieces such as we know them from the grocery store. He put the hams and bacons into a salt brine. The pork chops and roasts went into the freezer. Later, he would grind up all the extra bits and make sausage. But first, the pig had to hang for a day. The only thing Dad removed on pig day was the tail.

A pig tail is not really curly. It's stiff like a leather whip, fat at one end and skinny at the other. You can bend it into a curl, but it won't stay there on its own. You can roll it up and put it in a pocket, but once you bring it out it unfurls again. A pig tail without its pig is cold and rubbery and, yes, a bit icky to the touch in the same way that frogs are icky. Gross but irresistible.

After Dad cut off the pig's tail, he attached the fat end to a big yellow diaper pin. My youngest brother Jim was not too long out of diapers, so there was a good supply of diaper pins in the house. Once the pin was attached, Dad put the pig tail in his pocket and waited for his moment to strike. From that time on, I watched him like a hawk, because if you lost vigilance and became distracted over a game of rummy or Lego or race cars, you might find that pig tail pinned to the back of your shirt.

I don't recall if the pig tail game had a name, but if it did, it could have been Pin the Pig Tail on the Donkey, and I was *not* about to be the donkey. From the moment I came inside the house with ruddy cheeks and a runny nose and pressed my cold hands against the warm radiator, I had one eye on the task at hand and one eye on my dad.

I suppose at some point in my past I had been pinned with the pig tail; I was the oldest of four children, so I did everything first. But all memory of that early humiliation is lost. By now I was a savvy six-year-old, well aware of her father's modus operandi and smart enough to take evasive action.

The first thing I did was strip down. No bulky sweater or layers of any kind. A clingy stretch-knit top was the best defence – very little to attach a pin to, and even the slightest tug would catch my attention. Whatever we kids were up to, I sat with my back to the wall like a queen with enemies. Then I'd start an argument with one of my city cousins. Arguments were wonderful distractions. Dad could come up from behind on the pretext of intervention and, while pretending to pat an agitated child on the back, attach the pig tail with a sleight of hand. When finally my city cousin Bradley was successfully pinned, I felt more than a sense of relief. It was victory.

By the time I got that little red hat, many years had passed since I had eaten a free-range, dig-in-the-mud, eat-kitchen-scraps, bask-in-the-sunshine, carry-a-kid pig. Nowadays, most pigs are raised in mega barns with temperature controls, ventilation systems and grated floors so they don't get all mucky underneath. They eat a scientifically for-mulated diet fortified with antibiotics so they grow faster and don't get sick. The barns are bio-secure, which means you have to shower and change your clothes before you go inside because a disease introduced into this close environment would spread devastatingly fast. With any luck, germs don't get in and the pigs don't get out – except for that final road trip to the abattoir.

One fine November day, Art arrived at our front door with our pig cut and wrapped in two cardboard boxes. I thawed a package of pork chops, which we ate that evening for dinner with my homemade apple-rosemary jelly. One bite – just one bite not yet swallowed – and my husband and I looked at each other with a satisfied mmmMMMmmm.

Ordinary pork chops are good, but these were fabulous. How to explain it? It could be compared to eating a fresh garden strawberry in summer versus a pale watery winter strawberry imported from down south. Or a ripe tomato picked sun-warm off the vine versus a waxy facsimile purchased from the grocery store. Or fluffy factory-made bread versus the solid fragrant loaves your grandma used to bake.

Who knew? I was well aware that fresh-picked fruits and vegetables taste better than imported fruits and vegetables, but I was completely unaware that same principle could apply to meat. It was an epiphany over a pork chop. From that day forward, I vowed to stock my freezer with meat from farmers who raise their animals on a smaller scale, where sunshine and grass are part of the program. If I was going to eat meat (and that was not in question), it would be from animals that enjoyed a normal, natural life in the service of my dinner plate.

ONE DAY, MY HUSBAND came home from work and asked if I wanted to be an egg lady. My mom had been an egg lady. Every day, we collected the eggs laid by our chickens and Mom sold them to her friends in town for twenty-five cents a dozen. Before they were sold, we carefully wiped each one with a wet cloth because eggs come out damp and sticky, sometimes picking up a feather or a piece of straw. As soon as I could be trusted to handle an egg without breaking it, that was my job.

The henhouse was next to the pigpen under the roof of a low white wooden building that was, at one time, the first house on the farm. When the big new house was built around 1920 (ordered from a catalogue, like so much else in those days), this one was relegated to the animals. The henhouse had a double row of nests bedded with straw and covered with a wooden flap so the hens could lay their eggs with a bit of peace and privacy.

Every morning, we opened a little door to the yard and the hens wandered out into the sunshine. Then we opened the flap over the nests and carefully collected the eggs into an old paint can lined with straw. When I was really small, my dad took a picture of me gathering the eggs, looking rather cute in a red sweater and a kerchief. The photo won a ribbon at the Regina fair.

All these years later, my husband was not proposing that we build a henhouse in our tiny back yard in the city. But he knew this guy who knew a farmer, and every few weeks, that farmer delivered twenty dozen eggs to the guy, who then resold them to his friends in the city. But he was moving away and the farmer needed another middle agent in his chain of egg distribution.

We tried those eggs and it was love at first sight. They were the eggs of my childhood. Big and small, white and brown, lined up together in the carton like a mini-United Nations. When you crack one open, the yolk is as yellow as a sunflower. When you scramble them, they're the colour of butter, and when you make pasta with them, the noodles look like the pictures in a real Italian cookbook.

Those eggs were the beginning of a beautiful relationship because the farmer, Al Bennett, also raises cattle *au naturel*, pasturing them outside in the grass and sunshine. Al is a tall, angular fellow in a plaid shirt, silver belt buckle and tan-coloured cowboy hat. At a time when prairie farmers were told to "get big or get out," Al decided to ignore the advice and get smaller. He sold his big tractor and turned his grain and dairy farm near Meacham into a beef operation, raising cattle on holistic principles with no pesticides, no antibiotics and no grain in the feed. He divided his pastures into small paddocks and every day moved his cattle to a new paddock with fresh grass. The cattle eat the grass, fertilize the land with their "cow patties" and move on. In winter, he feeds them hay.

This sounds logical enough, but when he decided to farm this way in the 1990s, it was the act of a renegade. Most cattle are finished in feedlots, where they are fattened on grain, often with a boost from growth hormones and antibiotics. But to Al, it seemed illogical to feed his cattle anything but grass. Why grow grain for cattle feed when he could just let the grass grow and invite the cattle to feed themselves?

"Cattle are like the buffalo. They're made to eat grass," he says. "Why are we farming these hills with tractors? We should be letting the cattle do the work instead."

Al introduced me to his neighbours, who were raising free-range chickens on their farm. I ordered a dozen birds in the spring when the chicks were cute and yellow, and in the fall, they were delivered cleaned and frozen to my door. They were the chickens of my child-hood – big, robust, meaty and flavourful, the kind of chicken that makes the tastiest gravy and the healthiest chicken soup. Those dainty young chickens we buy in the grocery store seemed positively anaemic in comparison.

So there I was, reselling a dozen of Al's eggs to my friend Florence when she asked if I wanted to go halves on an organic lamb right off the farm. How could I resist such an offer? And that's how it started, one bite led to another, and within a short time John and I were buying almost all of our meat directly from small local farms.

One winter Saturday, as we sat down to breakfast sausages pur-chased that morning at the farmers' market, those beautiful scrambled eggs and Mom's raspberry jelly on my homemade bread, I looked deep into my husband's baby blues and asked if he would like to go all the way. We were already deeply committed, but I felt that both of us desired more. Sure, there's something to be said for instant gratification, and it's always nice to go out and buy what you can't get at home. But wouldn't it be more satisfying if we slowed down and really satisfied our natural appetites?

We were already buying a lot of food locally, but what if we went all the way? What if we stripped our diet of oranges and bananas, shrimp and peanut butter, Cheerios and basmati rice? We live smack in the middle of some of the most productive farmland on the continent. Surely we wouldn't starve.

So I asked John, "What would you call a local diet like that?" It was early 2005, before the terms locavore, foodshed and 100-mile diet had entered the popular lexicon. I needed a quick way to describe it. "Something that captures the spirit of the enterprise," I said.

He chewed on that for a moment, then offered a few suggestions.

"Monotony," he said. "Boredom. Privation." And with those words, I knew my husband must really love me. Because, after digesting my crazy scheme, he swallowed hard and said yes.

## 100 REASONS TO CELEBRATE

OUR YEAR OF EATING LOCALLY coincided with Saskatchewan's 100th birthday. To celebrate, I decided to recreate the luncheon served to the dignitaries that very first day. I acquired the seven-course menu from Saskatchewan Archives and pared it down to something more manageable and local. Gone were sweetbread cream, truffled sardines, kidney sauté, macaroons and asparagus (hardly local in September). Then I consulted a vintage copy of Fannie Farmer's cookbook, which was very popular in that day. My menu included cream of chicken soup, cucumber salad, tomatoes with horseradish sauce, lamb in parchment, potato bells, chiffon cake with champagne sauce (well, my homemade sparkling wine) and fresh strawberries with ice cream.

Paring down the menu like this highlighted how far we have come, in terms of food production, since wheat was the king of the crops. Thanks to ingenuity and science, we are growing foods never thought possible one hundred years ago. No doubt, the early pioneers would be amazed at the variety of foods produced on the prairies today. They would *not* be amazed, however, at the concept of eating locally. To them it was survival; to me it is revival. It's turning the clock backward and forward at the same time, following time-honoured tradition for a better, healthier world.

## POTATO BELLS

The menu for Saskatchewan's inaugural state dinner didn't specify the type of potato served, but I think this version would have fit right in. You'll need a melon baller. (Yeah, another use for the melon baller that rarely sees a melon!)

| | |
|---|---|
| 2 | good-sized potatoes, peeled |
| 1 tbsp | butter |
| 1 tbsp | canola oil |
| 1 tsp | fresh chopped rosemary (or ½ tsp dried) |
| | Salt to taste |

Using the melon baller, scoop out balls of potato that are flat on one side and domed on the other (the bell shape). Boil them in salted water until just cooked. Drain. Heat the butter and oil in a skillet on medium heat. Add the potatoes, rosemary and dash of salt. Fry the potatoes, stirring frequently, until they are crispy and brown.

# PORK CHOPS WITH CORIANDER MARINADE

Coriander seeds have a nice lemony scent. These spicy pork chops go nicely with those potato bells.

| | |
|---|---|
| 1 tbsp | coriander seeds |
| ½ tbsp | peppercorns |
| 1 | whole allspice |
| 1 | clove |
| 1 tbsp | brown sugar |
| 3 tbsp | soy sauce |
| 4 | pork chops |

In a spice grinder, pulverize the coriander, peppercorns, allspice and clove. Mix with the brown sugar and soy sauce. Spread a small amount of the rub on both sides of each pork chop, cover with plastic wrap and marinate for an hour or more in the refrigerator. Before cooking, bring the pork chops back to room temperature for 30 minutes. Grill the pork chops on the barbeque.

# STRAWBERRIES BETWEEN THE SHEETS

This elegant dessert can be started ahead of time, which makes it a great way to end a special dinner. This serves four.

| | |
|---|---|
| 5 sheets | phyllo pastry |
| ⅓ cup | butter |

PASTRY CREAM

| | |
|---|---|
| 1 cup | milk |
| ½ tbsp | vanilla |
| 2 | egg yolks, room temperature |
| ¼ cup | sugar |
| 3 tbsp | flour |
| 1½ tbsp | soft butter |
| ⅓ cup | whipping cream |
| | Lots of fresh strawberries, sliced (plus extra for garnish) |
| | Icing sugar for dusting |

To prepare the phyllo pastry, heat oven to 300° F. Cut each sheet of pastry into eight squares of about 4 inches. Lay the squares in a single layer on a cookie sheet. (You won't be able fit them all, so you will have to bake them in batches.)

Melt the butter until it foams. Remove from heat and skim off the foam with a spoon. Lightly brush the melted butter on the top of each pastry square. Bake in the oven for a few minutes, until the pastry turns very light brown. Watch carefully as they burn quickly. Butter and bake all the squares. This makes more squares than you'll need in case some break. Store in an airtight container.

To make the pastry cream, bring the milk and vanilla to a simmer on medium heat. In another bowl, beat together the egg yolks and sugar until light and fluffy. Add the flour to the egg mixture and blend well. Add one-quarter of the hot milk and whisk until incorporated, then whisk in the remaining milk. Pour the mixture through a strainer into a clean saucepan. Return to a simmer, stirring constantly. Remove from the heat and whisk in the soft butter a bit at a time until completely smooth. Cool. Press with plastic wrap and store in the fridge. Just before serving, whip the whipping cream and fold it into the cold pastry cream.

Place three pastry squares on each plate. Cover them with one-eighth of the pastry cream. Dot with strawberries. Add three more pastry sheets, more cream and more berries. Top with one or two more sheets. For decoration, place half a strawberry on top and dust with icing sugar.

# 2

# COUNTING DOWN

### THE 101-MILE DIET

------------------------------

ONE DAY WHILE I WAS OUT, the postman left a parcel card in our mailbox. The next day, I went to the postal kiosk at our neighbourhood drugstore to pick up the parcel.

"I hope you drove," said the postal clerk, "because it's a heavy one." She heaved a box onto the counter. "What is it?" she asked. "Books? Bricks?"

I checked the return address. Cerridwen Farm, Medstead, Saskatchewan. "No," I said. "It's lentils. Lentils and split peas."

-----

She raised an eyebrow, and who could blame her? Not many people order groceries through the mail. But when you're on a special diet, unusual measures are called for. And my diet was special. For better or worse, richer or poorer, fatter or thinner, my husband and I had pledged ourselves to a diet that was almost entirely local fare. For one whole year, just about everything on our dinner table – from asparagus in spring to zucchini in fall – would be grown or raised right here in Saskatchewan.

"Can't you buy lentils in a grocery store?" she asked.

A very good question. The short answer is yes. The long answer is a story. I used to buy lentils at the Saskatoon Farmers' Market, but the farmer stopped coming to the market and I missed him. So I gave him a call. I thought perhaps a little customer appreciation might lure him back, but, as it turns out, he was already awash in customer appreciation – halfway across the country. He was shipping his lentils to grocery stores near Vancouver where the clientele has family roots in those parts of the world where lentils are daily fare. For the farmer, it made much more sense (and cents) to ship his lentils out west than to drive more than two hours to a farmers' market once a week to sell them himself. However, he said, I could order them by mail.

Another customer had come up behind me at the postal counter and, since the clerk was expecting small talk and not a dissertation, I decided on the short answer.

"Yes," I said, "but these are local organic lentils. It's hard to know in the grocery store if you're getting local lentils because the labels aren't marked." I wrapped my arms around the box and lifted it off the counter, hugging it tightly. The last thing I needed was to put my back out carrying lentils to the car.

"*Bon appetite*," said the clerk, sounding rather more dubious than heartfelt about my next meal. I could not be sure if her skepticism related to the preferential treatment of locally produced food or to the notion that a lentil might be local to anywhere in Saskatchewan. If I'd had more time (and perhaps a soapbox, as there were now several people in line behind me), I might have told her that, in a mere twenty years, Saskatchewan had become one of the world's top producers of lentils. Every day, folks from Columbia to Bangladesh sit down to a bowl of lentils grown in Saskatchewan.

But it was early 2005, and the local food movement had not yet hit the social radar screen. Terms like food miles, locavores and 100-mile diets weren't bandied about as they are today, with food mile calculators, local food conferences and 100-mile potlucks as common as borscht. Back then, when I told our friends about our local food adventure, no amount of enthusiasm on my part could quite convince them we had not gone off the culinary deep end. While they politely said, "That's nice, but why?" their eyes screamed, "John, you poor guy, what has she got you in to? Drop by when you need a real meal..."

I decided we would start our local diet on the first day in spring that we could eat something green from the garden. From the vantage point of a brilliant winter afternoon, with the garden under a mountain of snow, there was no telling when that day might be. This uncertainty appealed to me. There was no X on the calendar. No "two more sleeps." No Last Supper. No anxious anticipation and no growing dread. We would slide into it as naturally and effortlessly as a breath of spring wind. Since we were already buying a lot of our food locally, we could think of it as a "spring forward" rather than a "fall back." More of a good thing rather than less of everything else.

Spring is the practical time to kick off a year of eating locally because, I was quite sure, I would need an entire growing season to prepare for the winter months. Considerable effort would be required to stock my larder, fill the freezer, harvest my garden, process sufficient quantities of fruit and source a myriad of other items required for a varied and balanced diet worthy of the Good Food Guide. In times of traditional agrarian lifestyles – that is, any time prior to 1950 – spring was the lean time, the in-between time when food supplies were running low and the land was not yet producing more. Unless we planned ahead, I feared our Saskatchewan diet might not survive to the following spring. Our hearts may be willing, but a weak stomach could lose faith.

The timing was also symbolic because I expected to derive a fair amount of food from my garden. It's not a big garden, but it is productive. We could count on salad greens, peas, zucchini, eggplant, spinach, tomatoes and green beans, plus enough dried herbs and frozen tomatoes to last until spring. The previous fall, I had planted a row of lettuce and radish seeds, which were now hibernating under the snow, just waiting for the wake-up call of spring, when they would sprout at the first hint of warm earth. If all went well, we would be eating baby greens from the garden by mid-May.

In hindsight, it's a good thing I didn't try to predict the first day we would eat something green from our garden, because I would have been wrong. That day came sooner than expected, a precocious Saturday in mid-April filled with the aroma of damp earth and the twitter of small birds who were just as delighted as I was to see the tail end of the snow. I had rediscovered the rake after a long winter affair with the snow shovel, and went to work clearing away last fall's leaves from the front garden. As I pulled the rake through the dead, dry remains of the chives, I discovered the tiniest, greenest shoots buried underneath that mat of leaves. The sheer determination of those chives, sprouting even though they could not see the sun, was a sight to warm my heart. I went into the house, grabbed a pair of scissors and cut them to the quick.

We ate those chives for supper sprinkled on a warm German potato salad, along with some *weisswurst* sausage from the farmers' market, my mom's pickles and Penny's homemade mustard. It was the first of hundreds of local meals to come, but first I had to break the news to John.

"Guess what?" I said during supper. He had already swallowed, so there was no turning back.

"What?" he said.

"Guess." I nodded toward his dinner plate.

"Is that the last of Penny's mustard?" he asked.

"Almost," I said. "But that's not it."

"We're out of your dad's potatoes?"

"Close. But that's not it either."

"Is this the last jar of your mom's pickles?"

"No. You're hoarding another jar in the pantry."

He looked down at his plate, spying those little specks of green on the white potatoes. "Are these chives from the garden?"

"Yes," I said triumphantly, "and you know what that means?"

"Oh, yes," he said. "Our year of monotony has begun…"

> Supper Menu #2: Hamburgers made with grass-fed ground beef, artisanal bakery buns, Penny's mustard, Mom's pickles, coleslaw and carrot cake

IN TRUTH, John needed little convincing of the merits of eating locally. Right from the start, he got into the spirit of things, conspiring in his own way to fill the larder with local fare. He went ice fishing. He cajoled a hunting buddy into "donating" some moose and venison to the cause. He did a bit of work in exchange for a fresh jar of Penny's homemade mustard. And for a small consulting job, he took payment in a bucket of Saskatchewan wild rice. You can hardly argue it was work done "under the table" when it squarely landed on top of ours.

He could also be commended for what he didn't do. He didn't complain when I stopped buying apples and bananas from the grocery store. He didn't mind that the cupboard was no longer stocked with peanut butter, canned tuna and white rice. He didn't ask for Gouda or Swiss and made do without store-bought cookies and soda crackers.

Sure, he was a wee bit disparaging at first, but that can be forgiven. On a gut level (both literally and metaphorically, I suppose) a local diet *does* sound a tad boring, but on a philosophical level it makes perfect sense. It's good for the environment if it cuts the mileage and the expenditure of fossil fuels. There's less wasted food and packaging for the landfill. It's easier to source food produced without pharmaceuticals, preservatives and other adulterations that maintain the illusion of quality, freshness and taste. It's better for your health because local produce is usually picked at its peak, so the nutrients are not depleted by under-ripening and long months in storage. It's good for the community because your grocery dollars stay in the local economy, sustaining smaller farms and processors. I welcomed the personal touch of meeting the people who produce my food, commiserating over the weather or discussing the merits of this variety of tomato and that variety of corn. Best of all, I love the way it tastes. Eating is not a matter of choice, but eating well is.

John already knew this because he is an environmentalist at heart. He attended the University of Wisconsin–LaCrosse, where several of his professors had studied under Aldo Leopold, that quiet, persuasive conservationist who had inspired a generation of young Americans to value the respectful use, not blind abuse, of the natural world. Leopold's musings about life on a Wisconsin farm, *A Sand County Almanac*, inspired John to build a little cabin in the woods of Trempealeau County, where he raised chickens, chopped firewood and lived off venison steaks and baked beans until a job took him back to town.

As a carpenter, he is a student of the Arts and Crafts movement and of the work of furniture maker Gustav Stickley of Osceola, Wisconsin. For Stickley and his Craftsman movement, the most beautiful objects are made by hand, not mass-produced by machines, based on a principle of beautiful functionality rather than cheap excess. John also admires the work of another Wisconsin son, the architect Frank Lloyd Wright, and the Prairie style, which calls for harmony between structure and landscape, using materials natural to the locale, with uncluttered spaces and abundant natural light.

These same principles, when applied to supper, challenge us to dine on fresh, natural, locally produced food rather than gorging on the cornucopia of worldly excess offered up in the grocery stores. In the Craftsman tradition, a recipe is a blueprint for fashioning fresh ingredients into something more wonderful than the raw materials alone, unadulterated by artificial fads and fancies, made by hand, and consumed with love. It doesn't look afar for satisfaction because the greatest rewards are simple and close to home. If food is a product of the environment, as it surely is, it should inspire in us the same sense of awe and appreciation that we feel when drinking in a beautiful sunset or admiring the delicate dovetails of a handmade chest of drawers.

Lunch Menu #3: Homemade bread and a bowl of ham and split pea soup

ON A CRISP WINTER DAY, long before the chives were stirring in the soil, I sat down at the kitchen table and made a list of all the Saskatchewan foods we already had on hand. It was an impressive list: grass-fed beef and lamb; free-range chickens and eggs; lentils and split peas; flax and flour; pepperoni and weisswurst; raspberries and saskatoons; applesauce and preserved pears; cabbage and carrots; wild venison and wild fish. In the spice rack, there were coriander, mustard and chili powder, and in the fridge were jars of jelly, pickles, mustard and sauerkraut.

Then I made a list of the things we would need. This included staples such as milk and cheese, pasta and beans, pearl barley and rolled oats. We would need more fruit such as cherries and blueberries; more spices like cumin and caraway; more wild foods including mushrooms and wild rice. More vegetables, more beans, more fish and more pork (having finished our pig with the little red hat, and our friends having divorced and moved off the farm). I would also need a year's worth of new recipes – recipes that made the most of Saskatchewan ingredients without resorting to the same old standbys week after week. We could probably survive on a diet of pork chops, baked potatoes and saskatoon berry pie, but that would only prove my husband absolutely right. Boring.

Brunch Menu #14: Breakfast sausages, fried potatoes, apple-rosemary jelly and for dessert, Prairie Berry Clafoutis

I MADE A FEW GROUND RULES. First and foremost, we would follow our local diet at our own dinner table and *only* our dinner table. We would not impose it at the homes of family and friends for fear of never being invited back again. And we wouldn't try to eat locally when eating out because very few restaurants cared a whit about local fare. (Fortunately, that has changed.) Nor would it apply to beverages because John was not about to give up his morning cup of joe, and while I do like a tumbler of cold milk now and then, I was not about to give up the occasional glass of wine with dinner. (There is now a vineyard in Saskatchewan, near Maple Creek, but since they sell out so quickly, I have yet to enjoy a bottle of their table wine.)

My third rule was the easiest to follow: I would cheat now and then. After all, the occasional teeny-weeny well-intentioned indiscretion would not spoil the broth. In fact, it might sweeten the pot immeasurably. So, for instance, if I needed a pinch of cinnamon for a fragrant Moroccan lamb stew, Worcestershire sauce for shepherd's pie, lemon juice for a salad dressing or raisins for bread pudding, well, so be it. Saskatchewan produces all the ingredients for a wonderful bowl of pasta, so why not make it truly great with a bit of olive oil and parmesan cheese? If the primary ingredients were entirely local, I would permit myself a few carefully chosen "foreign" ingredients with nary a pang of guilt. I justified these small indulgences on the grounds that our local diet was not meant to be an exercise in frugality and hardship – not a sacrifice, but a celebration of local food.

For more than a century, Saskatchewan has been producing food for the world, and I intended to find out what the world was doing with it. I pored over cookbooks of world cuisines looking for their dishes that could be made with our ingredients. Southern France and northern Italy were easy: tomatoes, peppers, chard, spinach, zucchini, eggplant, basil, oregano and thyme. Saskatchewan is one of the world's largest suppliers of top-quality durum wheat for pasta – even the Italians use it. From Germany and Eastern Europe: potatoes and beans, cabbage and apples, rye bread with caraway, bratwurst, *weisswurst* and a fat coil of garlic sausage. From Middle Eastern cuisine: lentils and chickpeas, yogurt and honey, cumin and lamb. From India: chickpeas and chicken, peas and potatoes, fenugreek and mustard seed. Saskatchewan is the world's top exporter of mustard seed – even the famous French Dijon is made with it. From Mexico: the "three sisters," corn, pinto beans and squash. From Asia: fish, pork, eggs, bean sprouts, cilantro and mushrooms. Pine mushrooms from our northern forests are a delicacy in Japan.

The possibilities seemed endless. Swedish meatballs in cream sauce and pancakes with lingonberries. Bolognese sauce and beef daube. Huevos rancheros and refried beans. Tempura and yakitori. Samosas and pakoras. Falafel and kibbe nayyeh. Clafoutis and apfelkuchen. Bangers and mash, fish and chips, toad-in-the-hole. As I collected recipes from around the world, it struck me how often the same ingredients, when placed in different hands, could be transformed into such diverse and authentic dishes. Even bread made with the basic ingredient of Saskatchewan wheat flour could be tortillas or naan, paska or pita, challah or baguette, croissants or scones.

Dinner Menu #31: Tonkatsu, okonomiyaki (made with fresh bean sprouts from my windowsill) and an Asian-flavoured coleslaw

HOW EASY IT IS TO TAKE the grocery store for granted. One grocery list, one checkout line, one cheery clerk who never fails to smile and call you by name as if you're old friends. One overflowing shopping cart, one wobbly trajectory through the parking lot, one drive home. One world at your fingertips. One-stop shopping at its best. One more job ticked off the list. One thing missing – local food. How ironic it is that, while Saskatchewan is producing food for the world, it is almost impossible to find the label "Product of Saskatchewan" in the local grocery store.

It soon became apparent that shopping for local food would require the investigative acumen of Sherlock Holmes, the astute questioning of Jessica Fletcher and the deductive reasoning of Hercule Poirot. It was not enough to read labels, which could be as misleading as a cagey suspect. A polite line of questioning could lead nowhere. Observation was out – who can tell by observing a bean where it's been? It takes a sleuth to uncover the edible truth, like peeling an onion or getting to the bottom of the pot one nibble at a time.

The fact is, most of the food produced in Saskatchewan goes somewhere else for processing and comes back to us with cryptic labels that give no indication of the point of origin. My extensive research (i.e., talking to anyone in the know) has taught me a few things about the food we eat. For instance, I learned that any bag of lentils labelled as a product of Canada is almost guaranteed to be from Saskatchewan because that is where the bulk of the nation's lentils come from. Any can of chickpeas canned in Canada must have, by law of averages, some Saskatchewan chickpeas in it. A package of pasta that lists the ingredient "Canadian amber durum wheat" is most likely a product of Saskatchewan because that's where most of the amber durum wheat is grown. A jar of coriander or mustard seed probably originates you know where, because Saskatchewan farmers have pretty much cornered the market on both.

What about milk, I wondered? Or cheese? How could I be assured of buying a dairy product that originated from a Saskatchewan cow? Unlike the cheese-loving cultures of, say, Quebec and Wisconsin, there is no artisanal cheese-making in Saskatchewan, at least not on a commercial basis. There is one commercial dairy in Saskatchewan, the Saputo plant in the north end of Saskatoon, so I telephoned and asked the kind receptionist to list the products and brand names that came off their assembly line. She gave me a phone number for consumer affairs. Clue number one: it was in Montreal.

I dialled the number and explained what I was up to – that I wanted to eat locally and would like to patronize their dairy products if she would be so kind as to inform me what they were. She took my inquiry and promised to call back. Several weeks and several messages later, I finally spoke with someone who could answer my question. And the answer was no.

"We don't give out that information," she said politely.

"Why not?"

"Because we don't want consumers to be shopping that way."

Detective Poirot would have been proud of me because suddenly a light went on in my head. What at first appeared illogical (you mean you *don't* want me to buy your products?) now made perfect sense. Dairy companies, like so many other food processors, have consolidated and centralized their production to such an extent that very little of it is local anymore. Milk is bottled in one place but the fellow who pours it on his morning cereal might be two time zones away. If I was eager to shop locally in my home community, where did it leave those local shoppers everywhere else? Switching brands, no doubt.

I called a dairy farmer, who provided another couple of clues. First, the major brand produced at the Saskatoon facility is called Dairyland. Second, each dairy facility has an identification number that must be displayed on the container. "In case there's a problem, it can be traced," he said.

A couple of trips to the grocery store and I deduced the number of the Saskatoon dairy facility to be 4015. There it was, 4015, on Dairyland yogurt, sour cream, milk, cottage cheese, cream and half-and-half. But no cheese. The farmer had mentioned cheddar and mozzarella, but I had not uncovered any cheese from 4015. I dialled the dairy again, this time after business hours. The man who answered the telephone didn't sound like he was wearing a suit.

"Why are you asking?" he said.

I decided that honestly was the best policy. "I live here in Saskatoon and I want to patronize your products, but I can't find 4015 on any cheese."

"That's because we make it here and it's shipped to Alberta to be cut and packaged."

"What's the brand name?"

"Armstrong."

"So it's packaged there and shipped back here?"

"That's right."

"So it has their number?"

"That's right."

"And do you know what their number is?"

"No. Why are you asking again?"

Dinner Menu #52: Homemade pizza with bison pepperoni, green pepper, mozzarella and the Bertolini family tomato sauce

YOU KNOW you're an old married couple when your ideal date is not a movie or a romantic drive or a bit of close dancing, but a trip to the farmers' market on Saturday morning, the earlier the better. Whether walking or cycling, we take the long way along the riverbank, under the canopy of elm trees on Spadina Crescent, past the art gallery and the gargoyles of the Bessborough Hotel, past the bandshell where wedding parties take their photographs and underneath the steel bridge that was built for Model-Ts, and along the water where rowers glide in the still morning air.

At the market, we buy coffees and a big breakfast cookie to share, and find a friend to sit down and visit with. We shop leisurely without a list, buying whatever catches our eye as the seasons roll through the year. We ogle the first greenhouse tomatoes, coo over the fresh asparagus, swoon for voluptuous eggplant and lock our purple-stained lips over sweet handfuls of fresh wild blueberries. Will it be walleye or sausages this week? Baguette or whole-grain? Asian flavours or sauerkraut? Temptation crumbles over berry ice cream, fat slices of quiche and silky fruity yogurt. We satisfy our hearts' desires, and John carries the heavy sack home on his shoulder like a schoolboy hefting his sweetheart's books. As a date, it's more social than going to a movie, more economical than dinner out, more wholesome than a nightclub and more exercise than a game of darts.

Dinner Menu #120: Samosas with tomato chutney, butter chicken and eggplant curry on wild rice

CULINARY DICTIONARY: Can (noun) – a sealed metal container usually filled with food. Can (verb) – the act of sealing food in glass jars in order to preserve it for another day. Jarring (adjective) – the linguistic incongruity of "canning" with glass, as in, "We canned pears last night. Would you like a jar?"

In the summer of 2004, John built a timber frame garage on Temperance Street in the shade of a big old pear tree. By the end of August, the tree was thick with small, green, perfectly unripe pears. We picked as many as we could without the use of a hydraulic lift (otherwise known as a cherry picker except, of course, when picking pears) and brought them home to can.

Canning is a lot of work. To start, you need to wash and boil your jars so they are good and clean. While they are boiling, make a syrup by simmering water with honey (sugar works, too) in a proportion that ensures a flavourful concoction without being overly sweet. Peel each and every pear, then pass them to your significant other to chop up the flesh, immersing the chunks in water tinged with lemon juice to prevent them turning brown. When a significant amount of pear has been cut, scoop it into the simmering syrup and cook for a few minutes, until it just starts to soften. Remove the pears with a slotted spoon and drop them into the hot jars. Pour in enough syrup to cover the pears and screw on the lids. Meanwhile, prepare the water bath: put a big pot of water on the stove and, using a canning rack, lower the jars into the water and boil for a scientifically precise amount of time based on the acid level of the fruit and the altitude of your kitchen, so that the lids are vacuum sealed and any trace pathogen has been vanquished. Oh, and did I mention, this task is usually undertaken in the heat of the summer, so that your kitchen becomes a sauna and you are craving your own water bath – cold.

Having mastered the art of canning, and having undertaken a year of local eating, I went hog wild. I "jarred" not only pears but raspberries, saskatoons, rhubarb and fruit compote (pears, apples, sour cherries and teeny tiny grapes). I "jarred" corn relish and apple-rosemary jelly. I "jarred" pickled asparagus and marinated mushrooms (which I kept in the fridge, since a hot water bath is not sufficiently hot enough for preserving low-acid vegetables). At the end of canning season, I took inventory of my stocks with a strong sense of accomplishment, confident we would not lack for fruits and vegetables through the long dark winter months. Then I put away my canning supplies and swore I would never do *that* again. It was too much work.

And then it was January, with its swirling snows and scant hours of sunlight, the happy holiday season behind us and the prospect of spring a distant longing, when we cracked open a jar of pears and ate them slowly, drenched in syrup and summer. I felt the craving of a lover separated, the ache of wanting and the joy of anticipation, when I would again feel the touch of sunlight filtered through the dappled leaves, and smell the grass and mint and warm compost. And I knew that come summer, I would feel this same craving for a blustery cold day in January warmed by a fire and a bowl of hand-picked pears drenched in honey syrup. And I knew, in my heart of hearts, my canning days were far from over.

Supper menu # 312: Pork loin with cherry sauce, wild rice pilaf and a bowl of canned pears

THE 100-MILE DIET is a revolutionary concept, but such strict limits are not for me. From the start, I was motivated by an appetite for healthier, tastier and socially connected food, with an eye on the local market and not the odometer. Saskatchewan is so vast in terms of size and production – it covers almost half the cultivated farmland in Canada – that arbitrary boundaries are sure to exclude more than they would include. Should I give up lentils from Medstead (140 miles), blueberries from St. Walburg (160 miles), mushrooms from La Ronge (225 miles), or pearl barley from Estevan (almost 300 miles)? After one leisurely drive from my house in the city to the family farm, my odometer, I couldn't help but notice, reported 163 kilometres – a pleasant and productive 101 miles.

## MEDITERRANEAN DIET À LA SASKATCHEWAN

ONE YEAR, I gave my mom a package of basil seeds and asked her to grow some for me on the farm. I had fallen in love with the Mediterranean Diet, and for that I would need a lot of basil. The word "basil" comes from the Greek word for "king," and there is hardly a fresh summer recipe from Mediterranean cookbooks that doesn't call for this King of Herbs.

Like everyone else, I had read glowing reports in the popular press which said the Mediterranean Diet is good for your health. It is why, we are told, people in countries like France, Italy, Greece and Spain live longer, with fewer ailments and extra pounds around the middle, than we do here in North America. And just my luck – many of the key ingredients in the Mediterranean Diet grow very well in my back yard.

Basil seemed right at home in my little city garden, but I had no idea if it would prosper in the big unsheltered, unwatered, prairie garden on the farm. But, toward the end of July, Mom called to say my basil was at the peak of perfection and ready to be picked. Since she and Dad were coming to the city, she offered to bring it to me.

"How much do you want?" she asked.

"A couple bags should be good to start," I said. I planned to make pesto, in which basil is the main ingredient.

Mom came to my door empty-handed. "Go help your dad bring in the basil," she said.

He was standing by the open trunk of the car. Inside, there were not two, but three big, black, overstuffed garbage bags. Turns out, basil grows very well indeed on the prairies.

# SUMMER RAIN SOUP

It is important to pick the vegetables in the rain. Somehow, the soup just tastes better.

| | |
|---|---|
| 1 tsp | butter |
| 2 tsp | olive or canola oil |
| ½ | small onion, sliced paper thin and chopped |
| 1 | small garlic, finely chopped |
| | A mix of vegetables as available in the garden |
| 1 | banana pepper, chopped |
| 1 | baby eggplant, sliced |
| 8 | green beans, chopped |
| 4 cups | water |
| 3 | baby zucchini, sliced |
| 3–4 | tomatoes, chopped in bite-sized pieces |
| | Handful of fresh basil |
| | Salt and pepper |
| ½ cup | couscous |

In a saucepan, melt the butter with the oil on medium heat. Sauté the onion and garlic until soft. Add the pepper, eggplant and green beans. Cook, stirring, sprinkling with a bit of salt and a few grinds of pepper.

When the vegetables are soft, but far from mushy, add the water along with the zucchini and tomatoes. Bring to a simmer and cook until the zucchini and tomatoes are just cooked. Scrunch up the basil, slice into ribbons and drop it into the water. Taste and add more seasoning if needed.

In the meantime, cook the couscous following package directions. Ladle the soup into bowls, place a spoonful of couscous in the centre of the soup, sprinkle with fresh basil and enjoy that lovely summer rain.

# CHICKPEA BREAD

One of the best reasons to work at home is that you can make bread any time the mood strikes. And the mood often strikes on a rainy day.

DOUGH

| | |
|---|---|
| 1 tsp | yeast |
| ½ cup | warm water |
| 2 cups | all purpose flour |
| ½ tsp | salt |
| ¾ cup | warm water |

TOPPING

| | |
|---|---|
| 1 tbsp | cumin seeds |
| 3 tbsp | coarse salt |
| 1 | small can chickpeas, drained |
| ¼ cup | olive oil |

Sprinkle the yeast into ½ cup of warm water and set aside a few minutes until foamy. Blend the four and salt in a mixing bowl. Mix the frothy yeast into the flour with ¾ cup of warm water. Knead for about eight minutes, adding a tad more flour or water as needed to make a smooth, elastic, not-too-sticky dough. Place dough in a bowl greased with 1 tbsp of the olive oil, swirling the dough around so the top is oiled as well and leave to rise until double in size (one hour, more or less, depending on the temperature of your kitchen). When doubled, press out the air and spread the dough into a circle on a greased baking sheet to about ½ inch thick. Allow to rise again to double in thickness.

Meanwhile, heat the cumin seeds in a hot skillet. When fragrant and toasted, crush them in a spice grinder until roughly broken. Mix the crushed cumin with the coarse salt.

When the dough is nice and fat, poke the surface full of holes with the end of a wooden spoon. Place a chickpea in each hole, lightly squeezing each one to remove the pale covering. You won't need all the chickpeas in the can, so feel free to drop the rest of them into a pot of soup. Pour the remaining olive oil over the bread, spreading it with your fingers to cover the surface and fill the holes. Sprinkle liberally with the cumin salt. (You won't need all the cumin salt, so store the remainder in an air tight container.)

Bake at 350° F for about 20 minutes, until toasty brown on top and bottom.

## LENTIL AND CUCUMBER SALAD

One day, Mark Loiselle came to my door with a bag of Red Fife wheat, just as Al Bennett dropped by with twenty dozen eggs, just as Karen Dale telephoned to say my chickens were ready. When it rains it pours.

| | |
|---|---|
| 2 cups | cooked lentils |
| ¼ cup | green onions, thinly sliced |
| ¼ cup | fresh cilantro or parsley, chopped |
| 1 cup | cucumber, diced |
| ¼ cup | feta cheese, crumbled |
| DRESSING | |
| ½ tsp | *each* cumin, coriander, mustard seeds and peppercorns |
| 2 tbsp | vegetable oil |
| ½ tbsp | balsamic vinegar |
| ½ tsp | salt |

To make the dressing, toast the whole seeds in a hot dry frying pan. Grind them to a powder in a spice grinder. Whisk the spices with the other dressing ingredients and stir into the lentils. Make this ahead of time so the flavours have plenty of time to mix and mingle. Just before serving, mix the lentils with the other salad ingredients.

# 3

## TOUGH LOVE

### TILL DIRT DO US PART

- - - - - - - - - - - - - - - - - - - - - - - - - - - - - - - -

WHEN JOHN AND I GOT MARRIED we had one prenuptial agreement, at his insistence: I would never grow more than six zucchini at a time.

Talk about tough love. Zucchini is my favourite summer vegetable, for a number of reasons. It grows quickly, it's lush and attractive, the flowers are big and sunny, and it produces a ton of edible food (well, perhaps not literally a ton, though it may seem so at times). Zucchini is incredibly versatile in the kitchen, whether it's the size of a baby finger or a small canoe; whether it's a soup, in a salad, the

———

main course or dessert. Best of all, I love the fact that the flowers are edible, too. What better way to curb the natural fecundity of a zucchini plant than to nip it in the bud?

I trace my love affair with zucchini to a sweltering summer in southern France, where trays of bright yellow zucchini flowers were on offer in the outdoor markets and tender-crisp ratatouille was on the menu in cool cafés. We never grew them in the big garden on the farm, and I could not recall a single time that I had acquired a zucchini and cooked it in anything but zucchini chocolate cake. Zucchini was, for me, a vegetable of little consequence, unattractive and unloved, always a supporting character and never the main event. France changed all that. Suddenly, the humble ho-hum zucchini was elevated to *haute* status, exotic yet unpretentious, a culinary souvenir of those hot, idle, thyme-scented afternoons on the Mediterranean coast.

As soon as I had a garden of my own, I planted zucchini. I made great plans for my first harvest – a culinary repertoire of French and Italian zucchini dishes to span the seasons. Early in the morning, I picked the tiniest zucchini with the flowers still attached, filled the blossoms with a mix of herbs and cheese, rolled them gently in batter and fried them crispy and gold. When the zucchini were larger, but still in the bloom of youth, I sliced them into a frittata, or pasta primavera, or a pot of minestrone soup. Once the size of a wrist, they were chopped into ratatouille, or grilled with olive oil and rosemary, or stuffed with ground meat and thyme. By the end of the summer, I gathered up the last of the zucchini, plump and matronly, with the girth of my grandmother's rolling pin, and grated them for vegetable lasagne and zucchini chocolate cake.

Despite my best intentions, this zucchini regime had one fatal flaw. In my zeal to recreate the culinary ambiance of southern France, I had failed to recognize that I was not supplying a farmers' market or a small café. I was cooking for one, and no one, not even someone who might feast on zucchini three meals a day (which I did not), could consume the prolific output of twelve healthy zucchini plants. By the time my zucchini reached the matronly stage, I had enough to feed an army or go into the business of selling zucchini chocolate cake.

And that's when John came into the picture.

"What's with the zucchini?" he asked the first time he surveyed my garden in Saskatoon. It was August and the zucchini were in their glory.

"Do you have something against zucchini?"

"No."

"Good," I said. "You're having it for supper."

Cooking for two had the positive effect of doubling my zucchini consumption, but it seemed to make no dent whatsoever in the quantity of the raw material. The zucchini kept pace, as if sensing that the drain on resources required a corresponding increase in supply. It didn't help matters when, at the height of August, John and I took a camping trip to the Cypress Hills. In zucchini husbandry, this is the equivalent of leaving a pair of rabbits free run of your house for a month or two. When we arrived back home, the zucchini had not only multiplied exponentially, but had grown to a fat, contented old age. I believe I had discovered the origin of the saying, "Give 'em an inch and they take a mile." Or at least a foot and a half.

I gathered up the most matronly zucchini and stacked them like green cordwood in a cardboard box and placed it in the back of my car. Wherever I went – a barbeque or an appointment or coffee with a friend – I did my best to slip the subject of zucchini into the conversation.

"Can you believe it?" I would say. "The world-record zucchini is more than seven feet long!"

"Did you know that Mussolini's favourite vegetable was zucchini?"

"Did you hear the one about the vegetarian who had a zucchini stuffed up his nose? The doctor said he wasn't eating right."

And then I'd get to the *real* punch line: "Could you use a zucchini? Yes? Well, just wait here. I'll be right back. And while we're at it, how about double for nothing?"

There's a saying in rural parts that the only time you really need to lock your car is during zucchini season. John, however, had a slightly different take on the old adage, suggesting I put a big red bow on the box and stop locking *my* car. However, such underhanded subterfuge was unnecessary. One by one, and two by two, I found good homes for most of my oversized zucchini. The remainder went into a bucket in the basement, awaiting a future date with a chocolate cake or the lasagne pan. It felt good to be generous. After all, growing food for self-sufficiency is all the more gratifying when you share the largess with others. Which is another great reason to grow zucchini: their largess is made for sharing.

MY EARLIEST MEMORIES of gardening include my Grandma Ehman, who had an extraordinary green thumb. Her front garden on the farm overflowed with a riot of delphiniums and peonies, hollyhocks and poppies. The big back garden was a neat row after row of prize-worthy vegetables: carrots and beets, peas and cucumbers, golden corn and old-world tomatoes. Before I could walk, Grandma sat me in the wheelbarrow with her jars of seeds saved from the previous fall or, later in the summer, with big pale cabbages and freshly dug spuds. From an early age, I learned the finer points of vegetable horticulture: how to tell when the corn is ready to eat, how to pick peas without yanking out the vine, how to tell a weed from a radish at the four-leaf stage.

I can still see my grandma pulling a carrot and cleaning it, more or less, by rubbing it vigorously with the green carrot fronds and handing it to me saying, "A little dirt won't hurt you." This old wisdom is now supported by modern science, which suggests that exposure to microbes early in life may be good for the immune system. I recently read another interesting bit of scientific trivia: two key elements of our DNA (guanine and cytosine) will, under the right laboratory conditions, spontaneously form on the surface of clay. This has led some scientists to wonder if ordinary dirt might lie at the very origin of life on our planet. While I am not qualified to wade into that discussion, I will assert, with all my intuition and imagination, that I have a little bit of prairie dirt coursing through my veins.

WHEN I WAS A KID, my dad would bristle if we referred to the soil as dirt. He would say, "Dirt is what you sweep off the floor. Soil is where you grow food." After a morning of picking weeds or harvesting potatoes, we had dirty faces but soil under our fingernails. We washed the car when it was dirty but scraped the soil off our boots. Dirt deserves a soapy scrubbing; soil deserves respect. That's how you think when you come from a long line of farmers.

On Dad's side of the family, my Ehman and Fahlman ancestors were farmers in Russia, near the Black Sea in what is now more appropriately called Ukraine, who moved there from Germany at the invitation of Catherine the Great. Almost a century later, in 1893, my German-Russian ancestors sold everything and bought passage on a steamer to North America.

On Mom's side of the family, my Scottish ancestors were Leslies from Prince Edward Island. In 1880, Great-Great-Grandfather Leslie came out west as a young recruit in the North-West Mounted Police.

He was soon discharged for medical reasons and took up farming. On Mom's Irish side, the O'Haras came to Canada in advance of the great potato famine. My grandfather on the O'Hara side met my grandmother on the Leslie side when he came to her farm to work as a hired hand. This new homeland grew food but more importantly, it grew families.

My parents met at university – Dad was a farm boy who studied agriculture and Mom was a city girl with an English degree. They lived on the farm for forty-five years, until my brother Tom and his family moved out from the city. Mom and Dad moved to a house in town, just as Dad's parents had done before him. Tom is the sixth generation of Ehmans to farm in Canada; his children, Evan and Emily, are the seventh. Perhaps someday, they will grow their families here, too.

As for me, I have retraced my mother's footsteps to the city – I live just three blocks from the house where she grew up in the neighbourhood of City Park. I bought my little house in January, when the garden was under a mountain of snow, and when the snow melted, I discovered there was no garden at all. I took a spade to the back lawn, digging up the grass in small manageable chunks and tossing it onto the nascent beginnings of a compost pile. I spread buckets of crumbly old manure from the farm and hired a man with a rototiller to work the soil until it was rich and loose. With the first good rain, fat rosy earthworms wriggled to the surface, which is the best sign in the world that the soil is good for growing food.

However, creating my garden from scratch had set me back in spring planting, so I decided to simplify matters that first summer and plant just a few things that would grow quickly and voluminously with little care and attention, giving me the satisfaction of an abundant, productive garden without working too hard for it. This included, predominantly, potatoes and zucchini, plus a few store-bought tomato and basil seedlings for added colour and flavour. For years, I had been growing pots of tomatoes and basil on the balcony of my apartment, and so they felt like old friends taking root in my new home.

All in all, it was a low-maintenance garden. Sure, the tomatoes would need staking as they grew taller and the basil would require pinching when the flowers appeared. The potatoes would be labour-intensive for a short period of time when I set out to dig and clean them in the fall. The zucchini were the least demanding of all. No staking or pruning or digging required – in fact, no human intervention whatsoever once the seeds were in the ground. Or so it seemed. As I surveyed my budding garden, I had no inkling that zucchini, the most low-maintenance of vegetables, would give me the most grief of all – precisely because I had given them too little care and attention when they needed me most.

As winter settled in, and the last few matronly zucchini began to shrivel and turn yellow in my basement, I had to admit that, perhaps, too much of a good thing is not necessarily a good thing. If I established a rigorous program of zucchini husbandry, with daily inspections and regular pickings, and if I vowed not to abandon my crop at the height of summer, I could probably fill my zucchini needs with just six plants. In other words, I could take John's matrimonial zucchini pledge with no loss of food or face.

On the other hand, did I really want to marry a man who would set conditions on his consent? Could I trust a fellow who was already trying to change me, well before I said "I do?" What's next? Would he demand that I save no more than six used yogurt containers at a time? That I borrow no more than six books from the library at once? That I never keep more than six jars of mustard in my – er – our refrigerator door? Marriage is a big enough commitment without the added pressure of caveats and conditions. I was happy to put his name on the title of the house, but did that give him power of husbandry over the garden, too? If I took his pledge, would I be setting a dangerous precedent or proving the depths of my love?

As I looked at those last sad zucchini, yellowing and forlorn in the basement, I knew in my heart that John was right. I'd had my fill. Truth be told, I didn't want to see another zucchini until the next zucchini season rolled around.

"I've decided to take your zucchini pledge," I announced, "and to prove my commitment, I'm going to toss the last of these zucchini into the compost pile."

He glanced at the bucket of yellow zucchini. "They're rotting," he said.

"No, just a bit soft." I poked one to prove the flesh was still just firm enough for the side of the grater. "But I've had enough. Twelve plants was six too many."

I went out the back door, into the blast of winter air, and tossed those soft yellow zucchini onto the compost pile. I did not lament the loss of good food; no, instead, I celebrated the productivity and generosity of my little patch of earth. It was not a waste to feed my zucchini to the compost pile. They had come from the soil, and would return to soil, in good times and in bad, till dirt do us part.

IN THE YEAR OF OUR TENTH ANNIVERSARY, eleven years in my house and a few days before we embarked on our Saskatchewan diet, I made John his favourite birthday cake: chocolate with sticky boiled frosting. It was a pretty day in early spring, well before the rhubarb was budding and the compost had been turned. Two dozen tomato seedlings, which I had started from seed, were sunning in a south window. Outside, the snow was almost gone. Since it was his birthday, I cut him an extra big slice of cake.

"Enjoy it," I said. "Chocolate will soon be off our grocery list."

His mouth was full of cake, but his bulging eyes spoke volumes.

"Well," I said, "chocolate isn't exactly from Saskatchewan, is it?"

He swallowed hard. "No chocolate cake?"

"Afraid not."

"For a whole year?"

"Afraid so. Unless..." I thought ahead to gardening season. "Unless, perhaps, it's a zucchini chocolate cake. If it's mostly local flour and eggs and zucchini, perhaps we could justify a bit of imported cocoa."

The relief on his face was visible.

"Given that," I said, "perhaps you'd like to release me from my zucchini pledge. It could mean more cake."

His mouth was full again, but his eyes spoke volumes. No. Well, it was a good try. In ten years of marriage, I had not once attempted to subvert my zucchini pledge, and that might be credited, in some small way, to ten years of wedded bliss. Sure, we had our share of disagreements and frictions, but zucchini wasn't one of them. Some couples may argue about everything from A to Z, but not us; Z was safely off limits.

My gardening philosophy had evolved too. That first summer, my garden was quick and dirty (no offence, Dad). The next summer, I diversified, planting a smaller amount of a greater variety: spinach and chard, radishes and onions, beets and green beans, cabbage and carrots, tomatoes and peppers, zucchini and winter squash. If the output of my first garden could be compared to a downpour, then the output of the second could be described as scattered showers. One concentrated to the point of deluge and the other spread so thinly it left me wanting more of everything.

But here it was, a decade since I had turned the sod, and I had found a happy equilibrium in the form of a traditional kitchen garden: planted primarily with vegetables designed to be picked and eaten the same day, perhaps even the same hour (or, in the case of fresh peas, the same minute) at the expense of vegetables meant to be stored for later consumption. Since my dad was still growing enough potatoes for a battalion, there was little to be gained by planting them myself. At the same time, the Saskatoon Farmers' Market had grown from a summertime attraction to a year-round grocery, with well-preserved root vegetables and hothouse produce into the winter months. If I concentrated on fresh eating, we could live off the garden in summertime and still eat locally for the rest of the year.

There were two exceptions to this kitchen garden rule: tomatoes and herbs. They are, of course, prime for fresh summer eating, but I like to grow enough for winter dining, too. In summer, I trim the herbs as needed for dinner and, come fall, the remainder are hung up to dry, then crumbled into cans. As for tomatoes, I put a dozen bags of Romas into the freezer (trimming off the stem end and freezing them whole) to supply a winter's worth of pasta sauces and soups. If I time it just right, we consume the last bag of frozen tomatoes just as the greenhouse tomatoes begin arriving at the farmers' market sometime in spring. With this annual rotation between garden and market, we manage to satisfy our culinary needs without buying a single supermarket tomato, fresh or canned.

Thus we had established an effective system of vegetable procurement well before embarking on our year of eating locally. For all other vegetables, for the rest of the year, we would practice a healthy case of denial: out of sight and out of mind. If it wasn't local and fresh in season, or preserved while local and fresh in season, we could do without. So, just as we had our fill of asparagus in spring, we would dive into spinach salads. After we had gorged on fresh peas, we would gorge on corn-on-the-cob. At the tail end of the peppers and eggplants, we would turn our palates to Savoy cabbage and butternut squash. And just as I grated the last of the zucchini, I would turn my sights, and my grater, on carrots and spuds.

IN THE YEAR OF OUR ELEVENTH ANNIVERSARY, twelve years in my house and a few days before we officially ended our year of eating locally, I made John a carrot cake for his birthday. He didn't miss the chocolate — or the zucchini — one little bit.

# PRIZE FIGHTERS

EVERY SUMMER, we entered our vegetables in the Craik & District Agricultural Fair. The rules were simple: each entry much include a set number of uniform specimens (usually six) placed on a disposable plate, clearly labelled with the type of vegetable, but not the grower's name, and deposited before the judges by 8:00 am on the day of the fair. As children, we took pride in our vegetables. It seemed only natural to show them off.

On the morning of the fair, we took great care in picking and cleaning our produce. It was important not to scratch the skin of a potato, or remove the little leafy stem at the top of a pea pod, or leave bits of soil in the hairy roots of an onion. We always picked more than we needed in order to have the pick of the crop. Six peas of uniform girth.

Six carrots of the same length, including the long thin root. Six matching cucumbers that would otherwise become six matching pickles. A near identical sextuplet of new potatoes. And six fat, perfect raspberries lined up on the plate two by two, as if waiting to join a parade.

We always won ribbons for our vegetables. Today, when I go into my garden to pick a bowl of cherry tomatoes, or a handful of peas, or baby zucchini with their golden flowers still attached, I can't help but line them up on the patio table like vegetables waiting for a beauty pageant.

# ZUCCHINI LOAF

This is not a sweet bread-type loaf, but a savoury side dish for the main course or with a salad for lunch. I found this recipe in a French tourist brochure.

| | |
|---|---|
| 1 | BIG zucchini |
| 4 tbsp | flour |
| 3 | eggs, lightly beaten |
| 1 | clove garlic, chopped |
| 1 | handful parsley, chopped |
| | Pinch of nutmeg |
| 15 oz | gruyère cheese, grated |

Peel the zucchini, scoop out the pith and cut into 1/2 inch chunks (you'll need about 4 cups). Steam the zucchini until softened but not mushy. In a large bowl, mix the zucchini with the remaining ingredients. Spread the mixture into a bread loaf pan, smoothing the top. Bake for about 30 minutes at 375°F, until a knife inserted in the centre comes out fairly clean. At this point, you may wish to turn on the broiler and quickly brown the top. Cool slightly. Cut the loaf into thick slices, carefully extracting each slice with a spatula and placing it on a dinner plate. It's good on its own or with a tomato-basil sauce, and it's equally good warm from the oven or cold the next day.

# PASTA PRIMAVERA

Primavera means "first green" in Italian, so this pasta dish is tradition-ally made with the earliest young vegetables of summer. Of course, tomatoes aren't exactly early on the prairies, unless they're from a greenhouse.

|  | Pasta such as bowties or rotini |
|---|---|
| 1 cup | fiddleheads |
| 4 tbsp | olive oil |
| 2 tbsp | butter |
| ½ | onion, chopped |
| 2 | cloves of garlic, pressed |
| 2–3 | small zucchini, sliced in rounds |
| 6 or so | asparagus spears, cut in bite-sized pieces |
|  | Big handful of fresh spinach, roughly chopped |
| 2 | large ripe tomatoes (one yellow and one red) |
| 1 tbsp | *each* parsley and basil |
|  | Salt and pepper |

Cook pasta for four people. Drop the fiddleheads into the boiling water to cook with the pasta. Drain into a colander. Toss with 2 tbsp of olive oil.

In the same pot, melt the butter and the other 2 tbsp of oil on medium heat. Cook the onions and garlic, stirring so they don't brown. Toss in the zucchini and asparagus; cook until soft, then add the spinach, tomatoes and herbs. Season with salt and pepper. Feel free to splash in more olive oil to keep it moist and prevent it from sticking to the pot. When the tomatoes are soft, toss in the cooked pasta and fiddleheads. Cook until the pasta is heated through. Take the pot to the table and serve it up.

# DEEP-FRIED ZUCCHINI FLOWERS

Pick the flowers when they're wide open. If the zucchini flowers are still attached to their baby zucchini, pick very carefully.

| | |
|---|---|
| 6–8 | zucchini flowers |
| Canola oil | |

FILLING

| | |
|---|---|
| 2 tbsp | fresh herbs (basil and/or parsley, thyme, marjoram, etc.), chopped |
| 2 tbsp | Parmesan cheese, grated |
| ¼ cup | good-quality bread crumbs |

BATTER

| | |
|---|---|
| ½ cup | flour |
| ½ cup | beer or water |
| 1 tsp | baking powder |
| ½ tsp | salt |

Gently scoop the pistil out of the female flowers and the stamen from the male. Mix the filling ingredients.

To make the batter, whisk together the flour, baking powder and salt, then whisk in the beer until there are no lumps. It should be the consistency of pancake batter, not too runny and not too thick.

Heat canola oil to a depth of 2 inches in a pot on medium high heat until the surface of the oil shimmers, about 350° F.

Cup a flower in your hand and, using a small spoon, scoop in some filling. Do not overfill. Gently twirl the petals together to close. Roll the flower in the batter, then slip it into the hot oil. Cook three flowers at a time so they don't crowd each other, flipping them to brown both sides, about five minutes per side. When golden, place the flowers on paper towel. Sprinkle with salt and enjoy while still warm.

---

TOUGH LOVE

# NATURAL BORN PICKER

### IF THE GENES FIT, WEAR 'EM

- - - - - - - - - - - - - - - - - - - - - - - - - -

WHEN MY FUTURE HUSBAND met his future mother-in-law, she was making pies.

"I only like two kinds of pie," he said.

"Oh?" said Mom, her hands suspended in mid-air with a lemon meringue pie ready for the oven.

"Really?" I said. By which I meant, could this guy *really* be marriage material? If he's a picky eater about something so apple pie as *pies*, then let's get this sticky fact out on the table.

"It's true," he said. "I only like two kinds of pie – hot and cold!"

---

We both breathed a sigh of relief, and Mom said, "You're in luck then because I'm making one of each."

It was September and we were at the farm at Craik to celebrate my brother's birthday. The day was hot as an oven and the harvest was in full swing. My brother Tom was out in the field combining the wheat, but later Dad would spell him off so he could come into the house to eat a quick supper and blow out his candles to the "Happy Birthday" song. Then he would go back on the combine until well after dark. Such is the Catch-22 of a farmer born during the harvest – the only time he can really celebrate his birthday is when it rains, but no farmer would wish for rain during the harvest, even on his birthday.

Given a choice of birthday cakes, Tom always picked a lemon meringue pie. And since Mom is genetically incapable of serving just one kind of pie at a time, she was also making my dad's favourite, a saskatoon berry pie served warm with vanilla ice cream.

The saskatoon berry is a prairie classic. It looks like a wild blueberry, only it's purple, not blue. The saskatoon is not as sweet as a blueberry but it has an earthier, nuttier flavour, and it grows on tall bushes in full sun rather than low on the ground in forest glens. Botanically, blueberries are a distant cousin of the cranberry, while the saskatoon is more closely related to the apple and the rose. But like the blueberry, saskatoons are chock full of vitamins and antioxidants, which means they have been keeping prairie people healthy since long before the arrival of Florida oranges and an apple-a-day.

Way back when, Native people mixed saskatoons with bison meat and suet to make pemmican, a power food that would keep for months without refrigeration. They sold it by the sack-full to European explorers and fur traders, which quite likely makes pemmican the first processed food industry on the great plains. In the modern world, the pemmican trade has been admirably replaced by saskatoon berry jam, jelly, syrup, chocolates and, of course, a marvellous pie.

The saskatoon berry also gave its name to the city in which I live. Here's how that might have happened, according to the history books: In 1882, a group of colonists from Ontario had just pitched their tents on the banks of the South Saskatchewan River when someone brought their leader, a Methodist church minister named John Lake, some of the wild berries that were in season at the time.

"What *are* these delicious berries?" Lake demanded.

"The Native people call them mis-sas-kwah-too-mina," said his guide.

"Miss what?"

"Sas-kwah-too-mina."

"Sas-kwah-toon, you say?"

"Something like that."

"Well, it's a good name for our new settlement. Arise, Saskatoon, Queen of the North!"

Knowing, as we do, that these colonists were members of a teeto-talling temperance society who planned to keep their new community free of the demon alcohol, we can be assured that Reverend Lake had not been nipping at the bottle before he made such a spontaneous and perhaps ill-thought-out pronouncement. Of course, he couldn't have known back then that the territory in which he invoked the settlement of Saskatoon would one day be called Saskatchewan.

There's a joke my husband likes to tell his friends back in Wisconsin about a couple travelling across the country by train. They pull into a station and the wife says to her husband, "Go out on the platform and find out where we are." He hops off the train and asks the nearest bystander, "What is this place?"

---

NATURAL BORN PICKER

"Saskatoon, Saskatchewan," is the reply.

Back on the train, his wife asks, "So, where are we?"

"I don't know," he says. "They don't speak English here."

Several years ago, a plant scientist pointed out to me that saskatoon berries were indeed *not* in season when the colonists arrived in August – August is chokecherry season. I don't know the Cree word for chokecherry, but I am quite sure I would rather live in a city called Saskatoon than Choke.

Since John moved up from Wisconsin, I had been introducing him to all things quintessentially Saskatchewan. He had seen Scotty the Tyrannosaurus Rex unearthed from the excavation site at Eastend, tramped the battlefield at Batoche, sampled the pea soup and tortière at the cultural centre in Bellevue, stood for a photo with Mac the Moose in Moose Jaw (in a thunderstorm, no less) and, at Lake Diefenbaker, had learned the meaning of the classic prairie phrase, "It's not cold once you're in."

And now he had experienced a prairie harvest and saskatoon berries, both on the same day. Later that evening, heading back to Saskatoon after my brother's birthday party, I asked John how he liked his first taste of saskatoon berry pie. It was almost dark and the sun was a ball of fire on a burning red horizon. In the fields, combines the size of small houses were making their rounds by headlight. Dust and straw swirled like fireflies in the beams of light.

"So," I asked, "How did you like the pie?"

"Your mom's lemon meringue pie is mighty larapin," he said.

Larapin is the word his grandfather used to describe his grandma's pies. She had a little café in Harvard, Illinois, where her pies were famous. John's father Jack was a regular there, where he fell in love with the pie-maker's daughter, Alma. Alma's pies were mighty larapin, too. Like a good Midwestern cook, she was humble about her pies – in the face of praise she would modestly declare, "Well, it's not as good as Grandma's." To which, John would agree. "You know, you're right. You better keep practicing."

They took pies very seriously in that family, engaging in great debates over the merits of the six-piece pie versus the eight-piece pie, whether pregnant women deserve an extra slice (since they are eating for two) and the acceptability (or not) of eating cold pie for breakfast. In these matters, John was rather conservative. The first time he saw me eat cold pie for breakfast – still in my pyjamas, standing at the kitchen counter, eating directly from the pie plate – I'm quite sure he wondered if *I* was marriage material.

After I learned to make pies from Alma, I felt I had earned the moral authority to weigh in on the matter: a piece of pie is as big as you want, as in, "I'll have a small slice of each." Of course a pregnant woman can have two slices – it may be the only time when she can eat dessert with impunity. And no one lords over my pie, *especially* at breakfast. In my house, she who makes the pies, makes the rules.

But since pie was responsible for bringing together John's genetic material, I felt he could speak with some authority on the subject. So I pressed: "How did you like my mom's saskatoon berry pie?"

"It was okay," he said, giving his best upbeat inflection on "okay" but failing to sound quite convincing enough.

"Okay?" I said. "Just okay?"

"Well, it's not my favourite."

"It's not my favourite either," I said. "My favourite is apple pie." Ever since my first toothless taste of Grandma Ehman's *apfelkuchen*, I have been fondly attached to any dessert made with apples, preferably homegrown. Grandma was a natural born picker. Her birthday fell in mid-July and she used to say the best gift she could ask for was to spend the afternoon picking saskatoons.

"My favourite is apple, too," said John. "Then I like cherry or peach or blueberry or lemon meringue."

"It seems to me," I said, my voice rising, "that you like just about every kind of pie *except* saskatoon." For the second time that day, I was seriously doubting his potential as a life mate. Can you even live in Saskatoon if you don't like saskatoons?

"Maybe it's one of those things you have to grow up with," he said philosophically. "Maybe there's more to it than fits in a pie."

That got me thinking. I reflected on my lifelong relationship with the saskatoon berry. That I might even *have* a relationship with a berry is, I suppose, proof that what he said might be true. I had to admit, the emotional attachment went deeper than the pit of my stomach. Mere taste could not account for it. The saskatoon was part of my earliest memories, part of the fabric of my family, perhaps even part of my DNA. In the great debate over nature versus nurture, when it comes to the saskatoon berry, I confess to being under the influence of both.

As a child, I lived for that sunny Sunday in July when Dad would announce on the way home from church, "Get ready, we're going to Findlater Valley after lunch."

By "get ready" he meant: put on a pair of long pants, a shirt with sleeves, a hat and a belt, and ditch the flip-flops in favour of those sneakers that had not been worn since the last day of school. Mom packed a picnic and Dad packed a stack of empty ice cream pails into the station wagon, and in no time flat, we were on the annual expedition to Findlater Valley to pick saskatoons.

Oftentimes we can trace our talents and predilections directly to our parents. From my mom, I inherited the collect-vintage-dinnerware gene. From my dad, I inherited a talent for picking berries. This gene is, no doubt, related to that ancient survival instinct called gathering, the act of foraging in the wild for berries, roots, mushrooms, nuts and edible greens. Thanks to my mom, my dinner table is vintage chic; thanks to my dad, I'll always find something to put on it.

My dad is a terrific picker. He starts early, picks steady, eats very little and doesn't quit until the pails are full. There is a legend in our family that he broke an all-time record for the most cherries picked in one day at a certain U-pick orchard in British Columbia. The owner offered him a job. That's my dad – a picking machine.

I imagine that somewhere back in our genealogy – say a few hundred generations ago – Dad's ancestors were legends in their tribe for picking the most berries or gathering the most mushrooms or collecting the most nuts. They'd trundle off in the morning with their reed baskets for a pleasant day of foraging and return at dusk, baskets overflowing with good things to eat. Sure, the hunters were the heroes of the tribe, with their dramatic campfire tales of stalking wild beasts for days and felling them with a single spear, but the gatherers were the Steady Eddies who could always be counted on to provide something to nibble when the hunters missed their mark.

Like my dad and my grandmother before him, I have always loved to pick berries. I love being outside on a hot summer day with the buzz of insects and the scent of dry herbs and grass. I love the rhythm of picking, like a meditative exercise that occupies the body but frees the mind. I love that sense of self-sufficiency, of taking what Mother Nature so freely gives. It fills me with hope. A berry-picking bucket is never half empty; it is always on the upside to being full – until you eat them. And that, of course, is the best part of all.

"Everybody out," called Dad. I was already out of the car and looping the handle of an ice cream pail into my belt. Not everyone in our tribe showed such prominent expression of the foraging gene. My little brothers were more interested in chasing frogs and climbing trees than picking berries, and my sister would rather sit in the car and read one more chapter of her book. Even my mom, an auburn freckle-puss, would rather sit in the shade than stand for two minutes in the hot burning sun. She slathered us with sunscreen and mosquito spray, and Dad inspected his crew.

"Jim, get your shoes on."

"Tom, where's your hat?"

"Maureen, why don't you have a bucket?"

She groaned, "Do I have to? I promise I won't eat any pie."

"Ya, right." Dad could always spot a fib. "Everybody picks for one hour."

We set off in single file behind Dad, our ice cream buckets bobbing at our sides and a bead of sweat forming inside our long-sleeved shirts, with Mom pulling up the rear to discourage stragglers. At the fence, Dad held down one strand of barbed wire with his boot and pulled the other one up, so we could bend and step through without catching a barb. We followed a cattle path through a shady copse of trees, avoiding that *other* prairie pie – the cow pie – and marched down the valley into a thicket of saskatoons.

Early on, I developed my own foraging routine. First, I would find a spot that was out of sight of everyone else. I liked that sense of foraging alone in the wilderness, as if (sneakers and plastic bucket aside) it could be any summer in any year going back to Adam and Eve. Next, I would pick and eat as much as I could, stuffing berries into my mouth until my teeth were purple and I'd had my fill. Then I would drop one berry into the bucket, and then another and another, listening to the little tap as each one landed until there were berries falling on berries, which made no sound at all. By then, I was in the berry zone. I could pick until the cows came home.

From somewhere across the thicket came a weary voice: "Dad, is it an hour yet?"

"No. It's only fifteen minutes."

"Oh."

As the hour waned, Dad and I were still picking. We didn't quit until Mom called us for supper, which she set out on a picnic table in the Findlater Valley park. Dad and I would peer into each other's buckets like two rivals on the same team. Dad always won, of course, but I was respectably in second place. In some years, the berries were sparse, and it could take all afternoon to fill a bucket. In other years, the berries were plump and plentiful, like small bunches of grapes, and you could fill a bucket in an hour flat. Some years, there were no saskatoons at all. Dad always picked more berries than were needed for a year of pies. As every good forager knows, you may be picking for next year, too.

Years later, when Mom cleaned out the big freezers on the farm before she and Dad moved into town, she discovered two milk cartons at the very bottom that were chock full of saskatoons. This is, by the way, another modern adaptation of the foraging gene – digging to the bottom of the freezer to see what you've forgotten all these years. The milk cartons were labelled with masking tape on which she had written: "Saskatoons 1994."

"Mom," I gasped, "you have saskatoon berries from 1994?"

She shrugged. "I guess so."

"But Mom, these berries are older than your grandchildren."

"I guess so."

"Are they still good?"

"Oh, sure," she said. "Do you want them?"

I shrugged. "I guess so."

A skilled forager never turns down an offer of free food, and I was just as happy to forage for berries in her freezer as in the wild, whether John was fond of them or not.

The truth is, since his first bite of saskatoon berry pie, I had been surreptitiously sneaking saskatoons into his diet in the form of a mixed berry crumble or a berry smoothie or a bumbleberry pie, with nary a complaint. I believe I had achieved some success in this subversive attempt to acclimatize his taste buds to saskatoons, but I had to face the truth: If I was going to satisfy his sweet "pie" tooth over the next year – a year without Granny Smith apples or tinned cherry pie filling or lemon meringue – then I would need to find a local pie fruit that met his highest expectations. A Saskatchewan pie he found truly deserving of the word larapin.

IF YOU SPREAD OUT A MAP of Saskatchewan, you may roughly divide it in half, with saskatoon country to the south and blueberry country to the north. Sadly, this demarcation was not mentioned in Grade Five geography. So, while I was a youngster honing my foraging gene in saskatoon berry country, I had no idea that blueberries grew in wild abundance a mere six hours' drive up north. Someone should have told my dad. We could have left after church and picked a bucketful by suppertime.

Nowadays, saskatoons are cultivated – that is to say, they have been selectively bred for growing in orchards – which is a great boon to the saskatoon berry business since jellies and pies are less subject to the whims of Mother Nature, and a blessing for home cooks who no longer have to brave the elements to pick their own. Frozen saskatoons can be purchased year round in certain grocery stores or picked fresh in season at u-pick farms. You can even buy pemmican jerky made with the traditional recipe of bison and saskatoons (if a lot less suet), which makes pemmican not only the first but the oldest processed food industry on the Great Canadian Plains.

(That European fur traders and explorers practically survived on the stuff seemed to matter little a few years ago when Britain saw fit to ban saskatoon berries until rigorous laboratory testing could prove they were safe to eat. After all, millions of Canadians might be wrong. They should have asked the queen and her children, who ate – with no apparent ill effects – many state dinners while visiting Canada at which saskatoon berries were proudly featured on the menu. Fortunately, saner heads prevailed when it was pointed out that saskatoons were already growing in Europe, in Finland to be specific, on bushes that had been imported from Canada, and no one had questioned the Finns' state of health.)

Of course, blueberries are cultivated, too (although not as yet in Saskatchewan) and are available fresh or frozen year round in the supermarket. Some call this progress, but call *me* old fashioned – I prefer the wild variety. Wild berries have a special charm, not only because they are smaller and the flavour is more intense than the cultivated variety, but also because their acquisition is a matter of age-old wisdom, family tradition, outdoor adventure and, in my case, the periodic flexing of my genetic code.

SO THERE I WAS, doing the Downward Dog in a clearing in the forest – a little yoga to limber up the muscles for another day of paddling – when I spied a tiny blue berry clinging to a shrub on the ground beneath my nose. I had never seen a wild berry quite like it before. It looked to be a cross between a juniper berry and a saskatoon. I shifted my pose from

Downward Dog to Crouching Dog and took a better look. Call it instinct or intuition, I knew in an instant it was a blueberry. So, I did what comes naturally – I started to pick.

By wonderful coincidence, John was making pancakes for breakfast, cooking them in a skillet on a crackling campfire overlooking the lake. It had rained overnight, but the dawn was still and bright, cotton ball clouds reflected in little ripples on the water and the call of a loon echoing from shore to shore. We were somewhere north of La Ronge, on a small forested island in a big blue lake, canoeing with our friend Tomas and his daughter Magda. In the north woods, it is always a good idea to camp on a small island because it reduces the likelihood of being eaten by a bear. The same goes for the berries. They were ripe and ready. I picked a handful into the fold of my fleece and brought them triumphantly back to camp.

"Shut your eyes," I said to John. I dropped the berries into the batter. He opened his eyes.

"Blueberries? Where did you find them?"

"Back there in bear country," I said. "But I got them first."

Pancakes never tasted so good. I would have gladly picked all day, but as soon as breakfast was over, we loaded the canoes and struck camp. I have a feeling that Tomas's ancestors were the explorers of their tribe, always setting off on new adventures in unchartered lands, returning many moons later with fantastic tales of derring-do. Not the type to sit tight over a patch of wild blueberries. Besides, he had to be back at his office in three days' time, so there was little room in the itinerary for random acts of foraging. Perhaps it was for the best. After a couple of hot days, a portage or two, sealed in a baggie, sealed in the canoe pack, well, we might have had the makings of a blueberry milk-shake rather than a blueberry pie.

That isn't to say I wasn't wistful as we pushed off from the island and dipped our paddles into the cool lake. Unpicked berries are like pennies from heaven that no one has stooped to gather. As my father's daughter, I had learned early in life that a penny saved is a penny earned and that a berry picked is one drop in the pie. I pulled out the topographic map and marked the island with an X. On the map, it was barely a dot, and I soon lost sight of it amidst the forested inlets and islands of the lake. In my heart of hearts, I knew I would never be back, but that X would forever mark the spot where I first fell head over heels in love with wild blueberries.

Over the years, there have been other canoe trips and other encounters with wild berries – blueberries, lingonberries (a.k.a. low-bush cranberries), raspberries, strawberries – all of which were consumed far too quickly to ever grace a pie. No, if I wanted enough blueberries to bake with, Saskatchewan-grown blueberries, I would have to track down a more abundant and reliable supply. And for that I would not need a topo map, but a road map.

THERE ARE FAR TOO FEW opportunities for heading into the countryside in the summertime at dawn. The light at dawn is completely different from the light of day. It floods the landscape in dewy greens and liquid blues and soft butter yellows, like an oil canvas so freshly painted it's still damp. Later, in the heat of the day, the colours turn bold and shimmery like a beautiful Old Master that has been viewed a million times, but dawn is new to every eye.

That is, if your eyes are open.

Here it was, not yet six o'clock, and I was in my car heading northwest out of the city with my friend Laureen, who was still half asleep, curled up in the passenger seat with a big sweater, a mug of black coffee and her Sophia Loren sunglasses. Laureen is not a morning person (at least not until absorbing that first cuppa joe) and I prefer waking to my internal clock rather than the alarm clock. But if ever there was good reason for getting up at the crack of dawn this was it, a Saturday in late August, the day the early bird gets the blueberries.

Any journey through the prairies can be plotted as a series of dots and dashes connecting one Big Thing to the next. This morning, for instance, we would make a pit stop at the big red bull at Radisson, turn north at the giant Mountie of the Battlefords, zip past the replica windmill at Edam, wave to Ernie the giant turtle at Turtleford and end our drive at the pride of St. Walburg, the life-size replica of Count Berthold Von Imhoff on his horse. Personally, I have a soft spot for those Big Things that personify food and agriculture. Despite the vast amount of edibles produced in rural Saskatchewan, these are few and far between. Among my favourites are the giant pea plant at Bellevue, the huge hog at Englefeld, the world's largest honeybee at Tisdale and the towering Ukrainian lass who welcomes visitors to Canora with a loaf of bread and a pinch of salt. And to wash it down, the giant coffee pot at Davidson.

Fortified with caffeine and homemade cookies from the Red Bull Café, we were back on the road in no time flat. Despite the early start, there was no time to waste. We were on our way to St. Walburg – a drive of close to three hours – for the annual Wild Blueberry Festival. On this day, once a year, the town swells by more than five thousand blueberry fanatics who come for blueberry tea and cheesecake, the outdoor craft market, music and dancing in the street and the main attraction – for which I had uncharacteristically rolled out of bed at 5:15 am – an opportunity to buy wild blueberries freshly picked from the forests to the north. Depending on the generosity of nature (or lack of it), the blueberries often sell out in mere minutes. I had been advised to be in line before the clock struck nine.

We arrived in St. Walburg with minutes to spare, parked in a grassy lot and headed briskly in the direction of Main Street. In this, we needed no signposts or parking attendants to point the way. We merely fell into the stream of new arrivals, drawn by the strains of Elvis crooning "Don't be blue..." over the treetops. Say what he might, "blue" is exactly what we had come for and if I didn't get some, I would indeed be moody blue.

Main Street was closed to traffic in all directions, and the gathering crowds spilled onto the pavement. Merchants were propping open their doors and moving their wares outside. Up and down the street, their shop windows were tarted up with big slices of blueberry pie and smiling blueberries doing a jig and waving at the passersby. In the cross street, an Elvis impersonator was on stage singing the blues to a phalanx of white plastic chairs, and, in the opposite street, busy vendors were setting up their tables for the craft fair. An empty lot on the corner had been transformed into the blueberry market with nothing more than a row of plain wooden tables. On the opposite corner stood an old-fashioned clock tower with its big hand inching toward the nine.

In the few minutes to spare, the blueberry pickers were hauling tubs of fresh blueberries from their trucks and trailers and pouring the berries into large zip-top bags. Since the abundance of wild blueberries varies from year to year, it is impossible to predict how many blueberry pickers will show up at the annual Wild Blueberry Festival or how many berries they will have for sale. But to my untrained eye, this looked like it might have been a very good year. There was an air of camaraderie, not competition, among them as they chatted back and forth.

"Whereabouts are you from?"

"Good picking there, then?"

"D'you know so-and-so up that way?"

"What's a bag of berries going for this year?"

"Thirty-five dollars? That's okay by me."

Laureen grabbed my arm. "Did you hear that? They're colluding on the price. Is that legal?"

"It's a blueberry cartel," I declared. "So much for free market forces."

At that, the clock tower struck nine and free market forces were very much in evidence – and we were left standing in their dust. The first rank of eager buyers swarmed the tables, wallets at the ready. What price to pay for fresh wild blueberries? For the uncultivated, unadorned, unprocessed bounty of Mother Nature? For that bright burst of summer on a cold winter's day? For a Saskatchewan pie that is truly larapin? We fell in behind and quickly moved to the front of the line, purchased our berries and carried them directly to a cold pack in the car. Mission accomplished in six minutes flat.

We spent the rest of the morning exploring St. Walburg and taking in the other attractions the Wild Blueberry Festival has to offer. Blueberry cheesecake in the Seniors' Centre. Blueberry latte in the variety store. Square dancing on Main Street. The craft fair, a sculptor's gallery, the town museum housed in an old church. Sometime after lunch we went on a hunt for the classic blueberry tea, which (despite the fact that it's made with almond and orange liquors, *not* blueberries) seemed to be appropriate for the occasion. Finding none, we settled for a beer, a Labatt's Blue, in the local tavern.

On our way out of town, we stopped by the farm of Count Berthold Von Imhoff, a German aristocrat whose search for wide open spaces landed him in St. Walburg in 1914. His art studio looks much the way he left it, full of grand canvases in the style of the Italian Renaissance, painted to the light of a north window. The antlers of a big buck hang on the wall (he was an avid hunter) and a sign from the St. Walburg Milling Co. (now long gone) with a message as Old World as his art: "Use homemade flour and eat homemade bread." He died a pauper (it was said he never charged a penny for his work) but left a priceless legacy of lavish religious artworks gracing rural churches across the west (for which he was knighted by the Pope). It was also said that he had perfect perspective – no matter where you stand his characters are looking straight at you, as if they are engaged in a personal conversation. As if the Angel Gabriel might smile sweetly and say, "Eat wild berries and homemade blueberry pie."

OF COURSE, I made a blueberry pie and it *was* larapin, if I do say so myself. That winter, John and I ate Saskatchewan-grown berries almost every day. Blueberry pancakes and cherry sausages. Berries on muesli and mixed berry smoothies. Lingonberry muffins and saskatoon berry crisp. Strawberry shortcake and cherry pie. Dried cherries in a wild rice salad and pork ribs in a cherry marinade. Raspberry jelly and chokecherry syrup and homemade ice cream with saskatoon berry sauce. The following spring, John made an interesting observation. Neither of us had had a cold that winter. This was quite remarkable. He usually gets a doozey of a cold that puts him in bed for a couple of days and I get stuffed up at least once or twice and, come March, I often come down with a bad case of the winter blues. But that winter, he wasn't sick and I wasn't blue. All things being equal, could our local diet be making us healthy?

I did some research and discovered an interesting and uncontroverted fact: berries are better for you than just about any other fruit. They are chock full of vitamin C to fight colds, antioxidants to boost the immune system and flavonoids for the grey matter upstairs. Strawberries have more vitamin C than oranges and saskatoons have more antioxidants than apples. They are a good source of fibre, essential minerals and several more vitamins, which makes them every much a one-a-day as many on the market. And much easier to swallow than a pill. So, thank goodness I got that foraging gene, and Alleluia! eating pie can be good for you.

## BADGE OF HONOUR

CONSIDER HOW OFTEN A PARTICULAR FOOD has come to symbolize a people and their place: shrimp gumbo in New Orleans, fish and chips in England, sausage and pretzels in Germany, the beef of Argentina, poutine in Quebec, or, to bring the subject closer to home, saskatoon berries in Saskatchewan. When the legislators of Wisconsin set out to change the slogan on the state licence plate, "America's Dairyland," the most popular alternative to emerge from the fray was "Eat Cheese or Die" (a take on the revolutionary slogan "Live Free or Die," which graces the licence plate of New Hampshire). We might expect no less from a populace proudly known as Cheese Heads. I should know because I married one. The minute we set foot in Wisconsin, my first order of business is to find myself in a roadside tavern with a plate of deep-fried cheese curds and a glass of locally brewed beer. Then I know I've arrived.

# PRAIRIE BERRY CLAFOUTIS

Saskatoon berries are the hands-down culinary emblem of Saskatchewan, but increasingly our chefs are using the new Saskatchewan cherry when a local berry is called for. This recipe makes use of both. In France, clafoutis (*cla-foo-tee*) is traditionally made with cherries and served for breakfast or brunch.

| | |
|---|---|
| 2 tbsp | butter |
| 2 cups | mixed Saskatchewan berries, fresh or frozen (raspberries, strawberries, blueberries, cherries and, of course, saskatoons) |
| 1 tbsp | flour |
| 3 | eggs |
| 3 tbsp | sugar |
| 1 cup | milk |
| ½ tsp | vanilla |
| ¼ tsp | salt |
| 1 cup | flour |

Heat the oven to 350°F. In the oven, melt the butter in a 10-inch cast iron skillet or large pie plate. Do not brown. Meanwhile, toss the berries with 1 tbsp of flour. In a blender or food processor, mix the eggs, sugar, milk, vanilla and salt. With the blades running, gradually add the cup of flour and blend well. Pour the batter into the pan. Scatter the berries overtop. Bake 20–25 minutes, until the centre is set. Serve warm or at room temperature, sprinkled with icing sugar or a drizzle of maple syrup.

# BERRY MUESLI MARTINI

To give credit where credit is due – I got the idea of eating muesli from a martini glass while breakfasting in my white terry robe beside the pool at the spa in Moose Jaw. Sure, you could eat your breakfast from a regular bowl, but why not celebrate those berries by serving them in a martini glass? It's so pretty you'll take a picture.

| | |
|---|---|
| 3 cups | rolled oats (not quick cooking) |
| ½ cup | unsalted sunflower seeds |
| ½ cup | hemp seeds |
| ½ cup | salted pumpkin seeds |
| ½ cup | sliced almonds |
| 3 tbsp | canola oil |
| 3 tbsp | honey |
| | Fresh or preserved berries – saskatoons, strawberries, raspberries, blueberries, etc. |
| | Plain yogurt |

To make the muesli, mix together the oats, seeds and nuts. Stir the oil into the honey. If it's too stiff to stir, soften the honey in the microwave. Pour the honey-oil mixture into the oats and mix thoroughly with your hands. Spread the mixture onto a big cookie sheet. Bake at 200° F for two hours, removing it from the oven every half hour for a good stir. Cool on the cookie sheet and store in an airtight container.

At breakfast time, spoon some muesli into the bottom of a martini glass. Top with a big spoonful of berries and a big scoop of yogurt. Add another layer of muesli, berries and yogurt to fill the glass. Top with some fruit. Take a picture. Eat.

# BUMBLEBERRY PIE

This could also be called Jumbleberry Pie.

| | |
|---|---|
| 4 cups | mixed berries (fresh or frozen) |
| 1 cup | tart apple, chopped |
| 1 cup | sugar |
| ¼ cup | flour |
| | Dash of salt |
| | A bit of butter |
| | Prepared pastry crust |

Peel, core and chop the apple. Also chop the strawberries, if you're using them and they're large. Combine all the fruit in a bowl and toss with the flour to coat. Mix in the sugar and the salt.

Roll the pastry so it will have an overhang of at least 1 inch when placed in the pie plate. Place it into the pie plate and scoop in the fruit. Dot the fruit here and there with a bit of butter.

Fold the edges of the pastry over the filling so that it forms a rough circle around the pie, with the berries at the centre uncovered. If you like, brush the pastry with milk and sprinkle with sugar. Bake at 375° F for about 30–40 minutes, until the crust is light brown.

# 5

## HALF-BAKED

### A RECIPE FOR DISASTER

-------------------------------------------

MY HUSBAND SAYS I make the second best baguette in the city. I am not offended by his "second best" designation – far from it, since the very best baguette is leaps and bounds better than mine. The very best baguette in Saskatoon is made by second-generation Italian-Canadian Tracey Muzzolini, who has turned her family's bakery into a little *paradiso* of artisanal breads. Placing second to that is like placing second to Lance Armstrong in the *Tour de France* or coming second to Oprah in the Nielsen ratings. Second in this case is pretty darn good.

———

On any given Saturday morning in the summertime, there's a queue through the front door of the bakery onto the sidewalk of 33rd Street. No one seems to mind standing in line because you are guaranteed to see someone you know; nothing passes the time like a spontaneous conversation with an old friend while bathed in the lovely scent of fresh-baked bread. It may be the only lineup in the city that is a social event all on its own.

It wasn't always like that. When Tracey came home from baking school in Minneapolis, her European breads were like exotic birds on the shelf. With names such as *baguette, batard, ciabatta, pugliese, pain de campagne, pain au chocolat* and *volkornbrot*, these were breads that most people in Saskatoon had never eaten, let alone pronounced. Business was slow. She would make a couple dozen perfect baguettes in the morning and give the unsold leftovers to a soup kitchen at the end of the day.

She was not discouraged. Tracey is a true artist for whom the joy is in the act of creation, not the commercial transaction. It took a bit of time, but sure enough the word spread and the lineups grew. Nowadays, her baguettes are bestsellers. The soup kitchen is out of luck, and you will be too if you arrive too late in the day, when the shelves are picked bare but for the breadcrumbs.

I willingly admit my baguette is not up to those standards, but it's not half bad. Sure, the crust is not as *croustillant* and the crumb is not as *crémeux* as Tracey's. And I didn't learn the technique in diploma baking school, but from a Julia Child video in which she demonstrates how to form the long loaves by rolling them under the palms of the hands, how to slash them with a razor blade and how to turn an ordinary oven into an artisanal hearth by spraying the hot inside with cold water. So you might say I learned from the best. When my baguettes come out of the oven, the conversation in our house goes something like this:

John: "Are you saving these baguettes for something special?"

Me (fishing for compliments): "Yes...for you."

John (with his mouth full): "This is by far the second-best baguette in the city."

Buoyed by his mouthful of praise, I could imagine my baguettes stacking up favourably against any baguette made at home in a fake steam oven with a recipe gleaned from an overdue video from the public library. But wouldn't it be nice to have proof, some outside affirmation, an award even? I needed a contest, an old-fashioned agricultural fair where the local ladies earn bragging rights by pitting their canned beans and raspberry jelly and angel food cake against one another's. As part of my year-of-eating-local research, I had scoured the internet for food-related events in Saskatchewan and had found just the ticket: the annual homemade bread-baking challenge at the Weyburn Wheat Festival. A red ribbon would seal my reputation.

Many towns in Saskatchewan could qualify to host a Wheat Festival. Wheat was the lure that brought the first wave of settlers in the 1890s (including my own farming ancestors) and was the source of the first economic boom on the prairies during the hungry years of the First World War. Little towns popped up along the rail lines like beads on a necklace, each one no farther apart than a horse could comfortably pull a wagon load of wheat in one long day. In each town, the grain companies built wooden elevators to store the grain until a train came to carry it away. Ever since, Saskatchewan wheat flour has been turned into bread in kitchens and bakeries around the globe. What could be more symbolic of eating locally on the prairies than a good, old-fashioned loaf of bread?

Most of those old wooden elevators are gone now, replaced by giant cement terminals that handle more grain in a day than a little wooden elevator could handle in a year. The few old elevators still standing are a nostalgic symbol of times past, and wheat remains the sentimental symbol of the pioneering spirit that transformed Saskatchewan into the Breadbasket of Canada. Today, many of those former wheat fields are planted with peas or lentils, coriander or canola. Saskatchewan is still the Breadbasket of Canada, but it's also the Lentil Basket, Chickpea Basket, Pasta Basket and Spice Basket – in fact, you might just say Saskatchewan is the undisputed, overflowing basket case of the nation!

So, while many small towns and cities *could* host a wheat festival, Weyburn has claimed the title, and for good reason. With three concrete grain terminals near the city, Weyburnites can brag that more grain passes through their point on the map than anywhere else in Canada, outside of seaports like Vancouver and Montreal. Visitors to town are greeted by several giant stalks of wheat erected along the highway, so there is no mistaking the sentimental source of local pride and prosperity.

Historically, wheat is not Weyburn's only claim to fame. This was the childhood home of W.O. Mitchell, the celebrated author who captured the feel of the place in his novel appropriately titled *Who Has Seen the Wind?* It's a growing-up story of a guileless boy in a dusty prairie town, read by school kids from Halifax to Port Hardy. Weyburn was also the home of Tommy Douglas, known affectionately as the Father of Medicare and not long ago voted the Greatest Canadian in a televised showdown. He grew up in Winnipeg, but was ordained in Weyburn in his first parish, and it was here that he first ran for political office. As the socialist premier of Saskatchewan, he introduced universal health insurance in 1962. Local doctors hated it so much that most of them went on strike, but forty years later you would be hard-pressed to find anyone who thinks Medicare is a dumb idea.

Hindsight has been less kind to another medical experiment sanctioned by the Father of Medicare. In the 1950s, Weyburn led the world in research into the curative powers of LSD. The work was conducted by psychiatrist Dr. Humphrey Osmond, who ran the Weyburn Mental Hospital and whose experimentation with LSD inspired him to coin that grooviest of words: psychedelic. He claimed to have given psychedelic drugs to Aldous Huxley, which resulted in his mind-bending book *The Doors of Perception* (from which the band The Doors took its name). Osmond wrote this little ditty to Huxley: "To fathom hell or soar angelic, just take a pinch of psychedelic." And it all started in Weyburn.

Interestingly, and to come full circle, LSD in its natural form comes from a fungus called ergot which grows primarily on rye, another popular crop on the prairies. Ingestion of ergot has since been blamed for the occasional medieval plague and outbreaks of Saint Anthony's fire, the symptoms of which were sometimes mistaken for the paroxysms of witchcraft. Today, farmers know how to prevent ergot, LSD is created synthetically in a laboratory and rye is better known as an ingredient in Canadian rye whiskey and, of course, a good loaf of rye bread.

I BEGAN to visualize competition day. I quickly realized that the location of the contest presented a logistical problem. Weyburn is four hours' drive south of Saskatoon. The contest opened at 5:15 pm on a Friday, with judging at 6:15 pm, creating a small window of opportunity in which to get my entries in. The winners would be announced in the historical museum when the festival kicked off first thing the following day.

So, here was the dilemma: Should I get up early, bake bread at home and drive to Weyburn in one long trek? Or should I go partway the night before, to my sister Maureen's house in Regina, bake in her kitchen the next morning and make a pleasant jaunt to Weyburn that afternoon?

John raised the obvious pitfalls with Plan B. "Isn't it better to cook in your own kitchen? With your own tools and your own oven?"

I had to concede the truth of that. But there were other matters to consider. "What if I have a terrible sleep the night before (from nerves, no doubt) and I have to drive four hours to Weyburn on the verge of falling asleep? What if I have to pull over for a nap and fall fast asleep and miss the deadline? What if my car breaks down? Wouldn't it be easier for my bread and me to hitch a ride to Weyburn if we were almost there?"

Besides, I was quite confident that I could make bread anywhere, in any oven, with or without a recipe, even blindfolded if required. I had several years of bread making under my belt, ever since John bought me a Kitchen Aid mixer for Christmas. Many wives might clobber their husbands for giving them an appliance as a gift when something more personal or pretty might be in order, and a lesser appliance like a waffle iron or a toaster would have left me cold. But my Kitchen Aid was marvellous. It had a dough hook, and before long I was addicted to making bread.

I experimented with different breads from all over the world. Baguettes and bagels. Challah and focaccia. Pita and tortilla. Paska and naan. I devoured books about bread, the history and folklore of bread, the spiritual significance of bread and the story of the grain that gave us bread. I traced the path of wheat from Syria and Iraq, to ancient Egypt and Greece, to Ukraine (the breadbasket of ancient Athens) and western Europe, and eventually to the Great Canadian Plains. I pulled this research together into a documentary on the spiritual and cultural history of bread for the CBC Radio program *Ideas*. I gave a talk at the public library and taught bread-making classes in the neighbourhood school. The more I read about bread and talked about bread, the more bread I baked. I was hooked.

After careful consideration of Plans A and B, I decided the best course of action was to take my bread-making supplies to my sister's house the night before. I would wake up refreshed and ready to bake in her kitchen on competition day.

The bread contest featured four categories: white, brown, multi-grain and specialty. My baguette is made with white flour, but I felt it fit best in the specialty category. Then I could also make a standard fluffy white loaf and enter that category, too. To make both these breads extra special, I decided to use a fragrant organic stone-ground white flour I had recently purchased from the Daybreak Scheresky Mill near Estevan. I had been to the mill in the course of my work – to write an article on the "Energy City" – from which I returned with three large sacks of stone-ground flour, rolled oats and pearl barley in the back of my car. If the success of a venture could be measured in edible booty, the trip to Estevan was a windfall.

The day before the Weyburn bread contest, I loaded up the stone-ground flour, along with my big baking sheets, water spritzer, yeast and razor blades, and headed south. (I didn't pack the Kitchen Aid, since my sister had received one of those for Christmas, too.) It was a classic August day, fiercely hot and fiercely windy. In the fields, wheat grew tall and green, bending like a benediction in the breeze. As I covered the miles, I rehearsed the timetable in my mind, plotting each stage in a process that would have me out of my sister's kitchen and on the road with my warm bread by four o'clock in the afternoon. I could already smell it, the sweet smell of success.

There is no need here to string my tale along. I will state up front that my bread was a complete disaster. Even before slipping it into the oven, I knew it was not up to par. The baguette lacked a certain *je ne sais quoi* – a certain voluptuousness and charm. The white loaf was pudgy and soft. Sitting side by side, raw and pale on the countertop, they reminded me of Jack Sprat who ate no fat and his wife who ate no lean – one loaf concave at the chest and the other bulging in all the wrong places.

"It will still taste good," consoled my sister.

"The judges don't taste," I said. "It's a beauty contest, and my loaves ain't pretty."

What went wrong? I could blame it on the tools. My sister had warned me that her oven was "hot" and I had overcompensated by setting the heat too low. I had discovered too late that I had forgotten the razor blades at home, and there was no time to run out and buy some. I slashed the baguette with one of those space-age serrated knives guaranteed never to dull while slicing through aluminum pop cans, but instead of renting the dough like a sabre, it ripped like a tooth.

Or I could blame it on the timing. Stone-ground flour, no matter how silky and white, is heavier and coarser than any all-purpose factory-ground flour. It likes a little more yeast. It needs a little more kneading. It takes a little longer to rise. In the excitement of competition, I had failed to compensate for these elemental and foreseeable pitfalls. Running up against the clock, I had dashed the baguette into the oven before its time, and while it cooked, the other loaf over-proofed on the countertop. The baguette sagged and the loaf lumped. It was a tragic sight. I prayed for a miracle in the oven – not the multiplying of loaves but a complete rising from the dead!

Or perhaps I should blame it on my year of eating locally. If not for that endeavour, I might not have bought a sack of organic stone-ground flour at the Daybreak Scheresky Mill and might have employed plain old all-purpose flour for the competition. If I had not searched the internet for Saskatchewan food news, I might not have even contemplated leaving my home kitchen for the hubris of competitive bread baking in a foreign oven. And if I didn't make my own bread instead of buying store-bought factory bread, I would not be staring at two tasty but imperfect loaves on my sister's kitchen counter.

"I'm not going," I told her. "This bread is not fit for a contest. We'll have it for dinner and eat my shame."

But Maureen would hear none of it. She had taken the day off work to accompany me to Weyburn and, like any good coach, she was not letting me give in. "Let's go," she said. "Take a look at the competition before you decide. Maybe it won't be so bad."

We put the warm bread in the back of the car and drove to Weyburn. One glance and I could see that the competition was good – but scarce. There were no entries yet in the category for specialty breads and only two entries for white. As it turned out, Weyburn was overwhelmed that weekend with homecoming reunions and weddings, so I imagine the most fabled bread makers were busy baking for guests (or sharing rye in liquid form) to find the time to enter contents. The field was open.

"You've come a long way," said the woman at the entry desk. I had already confessed that my bread was under par. "The prizes are good. What have you got to lose?"

To lose? Only my good name. Only my reputation as a bread maker. Only my fans who listened to my bread documentary on the radio, or took my bread-making class, or read my food column in the newspaper and expected far better of me.

"You're a writer," said Maureen. "Use a pseudonym."

This had not occurred to me. But in a split second I could see the wisdom in it. I could enter my bread, thus not having wasted my time at the Weyburn Wheat Festival, and I would save face by doing it anonymously. I would choose a name to which I had a legitimate right, but one which could not be connected to me by anyone but a few close friends and family. I would use my husband's surname.

I signed my name, Amy Bertolini, and laid my bread on the judging table. The night before, I had sewn two blue tea towels into natural looking folds, like a Dutch still life, and carefully wrote two place cards in calligraphy identifying each type of bread. As I fussed over my arrangement, I noticed that no other bakers had taken such airs with their own bread.

"If nothing else," observed Maureen, "you get points for presentation."

I left the building feeling a bit more confident than I had all day. But there in the parking lot, in the shadow of the giant wheat stalks, my bubble burst. A sturdy woman had just arrived with a big cardboard box on the seat of her truck. It was full of bread. I looked at my watch. Almost 6:15. The competition had arrived just under the wire. Driving back to Regina that golden evening, my spirits were as flat as my sorry baguette.

THE FOLLOWING DAY, my sister and I got up early and returned to Weyburn. You might expect that we made a quick dash for the historical museum to see how my bread had fared. We did not. I wanted to enjoy the day before facing the truth, and the Weyburn Wheat Festival offered many diversions. First, a pancake and sausage breakfast in front of city hall, followed by a bus tour of the countryside. The bus was full of senior citizens who were in town for the homecoming. Other than a child with her grandmother, Maureen and I were the youngest two on the bus. Behind us, a couple of old guys commiserated on the vagaries of the weather: "It coulda been a bumper crop this year, but this heat and this wind, it's flattened everything."

"Last year, I woulda had a good harvest but I got hit with that killer frost."

"It's nothing like the grasshoppers we had back in... "

Ah, the coulda wouldas. If only I woulda baked in my own kitchen. If only I coulda had little more time. If only I woulda hadda proper razor blade. Unlike these seasoned farmers who had Mother Nature to blame, I had no one to curse but myself.

As the bus eased its way through the leafy streets, a tall twiggy fellow in a straw cowboy hat introduced himself as our tour guide with the delightfully fitting name of Norm Flaten. The countryside outside Weyburn was as flat as a patchwork quilt and just as pretty. Tall stands of grain waved like a great green sea and millions of little white butterflies darted in the clover that grew in the ditches along the road. The bus stopped at a horse farm and at a workshop that made concrete pipes. At each stop, we stepped off the air-conditioned bus into a hot blast of wind that whipped our hair and gritted our eyes. As W.O. Mitchell wrote, you really could see this wind.

The final stop was the Weyburn Inland Terminal. Standing in the shadow of those concrete towers, it was easy to be awed by their sheer enormity and the staggering amount of grain stored there. When the train comes to load up, it fills at a rate of six minutes per car, ten cars per hour, up to 120 cars per day. As we climbed back on the bus, a speeding train passed by on its way to another destination, whispering on the rails like a long melancholy sigh.

The bus returned to town, but our procrastination tour was not over yet. Next, a visit to the church where Rev. Tommy Douglas preached the gospel, and then a stop at the Weyburn Heritage Village, where an old-time fiddle band played on a shady veranda as we ate warm bread drawn from a wood-burning oven, slathered with homemade strawberry jam. A crowd was gathering on the grass for a celebrity stooking competition. Stooking is the act of gathering the stalks of wheat into sheaves and loading them onto a horse-drawn wagon, from which they are tossed into the old noisy behemoth threshing machine. It's heavy, dusty work. The celebrity was television host Valerie Pringle, whose every heave and grunt were captured by her camera crew. Amazingly, she won the prize. Must be beginners' luck.

The sun was on the downward side of the afternoon when finally we made our way back to the historical museum and the homemade bread contest. Several rooms of the museum are dedicated to the Weyburn Mental Hospital (I saw no mention of LSD), and another section houses an amazing collection of gleaming silverware collected by a bachelor farmer named Charlie Wilson, who kept it in crates and boxes throughout his old farmhouse. It's hard to imagine Charlie had much use for silver candelabra and hair brushes and salt pots – or that hefty sculpture of Eleanor of Aquitaine dressed in fine robes with a falcon on her arm – but perhaps he did use a silver egg cup or a teapot or a butter knife every now and then. When he died, Charlie willed his collection to the historical museum, which chose several thousand of the most exquisite pieces and put them on display – after vigorous polishing by a couple of summer students and a crate of Silvo.

It was, finally, the moment of truth. I sent Maureen ahead to take a peek, watching from the doorway until she waved me in with a smile. I had not fared so badly, in a glass-half-full sort of way. My bread had placed last in both categories, but since there were so few entries, I had actually won a prize. My baguette came second to a beautiful loaf of rye bread, earning a ten-dollar gift certificate at a local pizzeria. We stopped for a bite to eat, then drove back to Regina with a raging wind at our backs.

The next day when I got home to Saskatoon my husband greeted me at the front door.

"How was it?" he asked. "How did your bread do?"

"Not bad," I said cheerily. "My baguette came in second place."

"I knew it," he said, giving me a victory hug. "I always said your baguette was second best."

## FIT FOR THE ARK

BACK AROUND 1900, as the first wave of settlers began farming the prairies, they grew a variety of wheat called Red Fife. It was named for David Fife, the farmer in Ontario who grew it from a handful of seeds that arrived on a ship from Scotland, as the story goes. His variety of wheat was planted across the US and Canadian plains until botanists bred newer varieties (using Red Fife as a parent) that were better suited to our growing conditions on the northern prairie. Red Fife was largely forgotten.

Until now. Red Fife is back, thanks to a group of Saskatchewan organic farmers led by Marc Loiselle of Vonda. They've found a niche market among artisanal bread bakers from Victoria to Halifax who like the nutty flavour and heritage status of Red Fife. In fact, Red Fife was Canada's first entry in the Slow Food "Ark of Taste," a catalogue of unique but threatened foods produced around the world.

The trouble is, in Canada, Red Fife has been declassified as human food. This measure was taken so that an old "inferior" variety of wheat

doesn't get mixed up with the modern wheats grown today. As a result, Marc and the other farmers are required to sell it as animal feed. Of course, what the buyers do with it is nobody's business.

Fit only for the animals? Welcome to the Ark.

# FOUR GRAIN SOUP

This is a hearty soup for a winter day. For a vegetarian version, use vegetable stock or water. For a meatier version, add slices of farmer's sausage.

| | |
|---|---|
| 1 tbsp | canola oil |
| 1 tbsp | butter |
| 1 | onion, chopped |
| 2 | carrots, diced |
| 1 tsp | dried thyme |
| | Salt and pepper |
| ⅓ cup | *each* lentils, Red Fife wheat seeds, pearl barley, and wild rice |
| 1 | 540-ml can chopped tomatoes (or 10 garden tomatoes) |
| 6 cups | chicken stock |

Heat canola oil and butter in a soup pot on medium heat. Sauté the onions and carrots until softened, then stir in the dried thyme, salt and pepper. Add the four grains: lentils, wheat, barley and wild rice. Turn up heat to medium high and cook, stirring frequently, until the grains are shiny and starting to stick to the pot. Add tomatoes (with their juice) and stock. Bring to a boil. Reduce heat and simmer with the lid on until the grains are soft, about 45 minutes. Taste before serving, adding more salt and pepper as needed. Serve with crusty bread.

# BLT IN A BOWL

Bread salads are very popular in some parts of the world and are a great way to use up good bread that's turned dry.

| | |
|---|---|
| 4 | slices bacon |
| 3 | slices day-old bread |
| 2 | red tomatoes |
| 2 cups | salad greens |

DRESSING

| | |
|---|---|
| 2 tbsp | mayonnaise |
| ½ tsp | Dijon mustard |
| 2 ½ tsp | milk |
| | Salt and pepper |

Fry the bacon until crisp. Drain on paper towel and crumble when cool. Trim the bread of crusts. Toast lightly and cut into bite-sized cubes.

Chop the tomatoes. Place in a serving bowl, squeezing gently to release some juices.

Whisk together the dressing ingredients. Pour onto the tomatoes and stir. A few minutes before serving, add the bread and bacon to the tomatoes and toss well. You want to give the bread time to soak up some dressing, but not so long that it gets mushy.

Arrange the salad greens on two plates. Spoon the tomato-bread mixture onto the greens. Enjoy your BLT with a fork!

# LENTIL SPROUT WRAPS

You have to start this sandwich five days before lunch. How's that for planning! The only "equipment" you need is a big jar and a piece of cheesecloth or loose-weave fabric.

SPROUTS

| | |
|---|---|
| ¼ cup | whole lentils (any dried – not canned – lentil will do) |
| | A big jar with a piece of cheesecloth or loose-weave fabric |
| | Elastic band |

SALAD

| | |
|---|---|
| 2 tsp | minced onion |
| 2 tbsp | mayonnaise |
| 1 tbsp | plain yogurt |
| ¼ tsp | *each* ground cumin and coriander |
| | Dash of salt and a few grinds of pepper |
| ½ cup | lentil sprouts |
| 3 | hard-cooked eggs, chopped |
| 3 | whole wheat tortilla wraps |

Place the lentils in the jar, cover generously with water and fix the cheesecloth or other loosely woven fabric over top with an elastic band. After four hours, drain the water through the cheesecloth. Place the jar on its side, shaking to spread the lentils and set on a sunny kitchen counter. Twice a day, add water, swirl briefly and drain, placing the jar back in the sun. In five days, you'll have sprouts.

Mix together all the salad ingredients. Divide between three whole wheat wraps. Roll and enjoy.

---

# 6

# THE MOREL OF THE STORY

## DEFYING DEATH IN MUSHROOM COUNTRY

ONE OF THE MYSTERIES of my childhood was the mushroom. For the most part, mushrooms came out of a can – but rarely, because as children we were not very fond of them. It seemed the height of ridiculous to spoil a perfectly good meal, say pasta with meat sauce or a pepperoni pizza, by adding an ingredient that could best be described as rubbery, grey and slick. Of course, canned mushrooms were guaranteed not to be poisonous, but they *were* certifiably noxious. Not much of a trade off, as far as I was concerned.

Occasionally, during a particularly wet summer, wild mushrooms popped up mysteriously all over the farm. Black feathery mushrooms at the edge of the garden, white toadstools under the climbing tree, fairy rings in the grass. As children, we were allowed to play with the mushrooms. That is to say, we had permission to stomp them, throw them, whack them with golf clubs and baseball bats, even dissect them with a kitchen knife and view them under the microscope (provided we thoroughly washed the knife and our fingers afterward). The one thing we were not permitted to do with a wild mushroom was eat it. Wild mushrooms were strictly *not* food.

Then would come the day that Dad walked into the kitchen with a passel of wild mushrooms scooped up in the folds of his work shirt. He wiped them, chopped them and, while we observed at a safe distance, cooked them in plenty of butter. It looked, for all intents and purposes, as if he were planning to eat them.

"Not in front of the kids," said Mom.

We were whisked out of the kitchen, the lovely scent of buttery mushrooms trailing on the air, to wait sight unseen with our stomachs rumbling until Dad had finished his homegrown hors d'oeuvres in solitude. No doubt Mom was worried we might copy Dad's example without the corresponding knowledge of which mushrooms were safe to eat. I suspect she was also worried that even *he* didn't know which mushrooms were safe to eat. While she had resigned herself to the possibility of losing her husband to a poisonous mushroom, she was not willing to risk that we might witness our father's demise in a fit of paroxysms on the kitchen floor.

It worked. Thanks to her diligence, and the occasional can of mushrooms, I was frightened and repulsed in equal measure. I survived childhood devoid of any inclination to experiment behind her back. It was not until years later, when I was cooking for myself, that I became acquainted with Mother Nature's antidote to mushroom phobia: those small white button mushrooms, *Agaricus bisporus*, which had so conveniently popped up in the grocery stores. In France they are called *champignon de Paris* and in Italy they're known as *cremini* or, when grown very large, *portobello*. Whether addressed in English, Latin, French or Italian, it was a mushroom guaranteed to taste good without threatening your life.

To the delight of my taste buds, I discovered that I shared my father's love of fresh mushrooms sautéed in butter. As my mother's daughter, I still harboured deep-seated suspicions of the wild variety, but what did it matter now that safe, cultivated mushrooms were easy pickings in the grocery store? I dined on store-bought mushrooms with carefree impunity, never giving their wild cousins a second thought. No second thought whatsoever – until that fateful day I turned my culinary world inside out by pledging to eat local foods for one whole year. Up till then, I had never seen fresh Saskatchewan mushrooms for sale in a grocery store, and they were not on offer at the farmers' market. If I was going to enjoy mushrooms during the course of those 365 days, I decided the best course of action was to go out and pick them myself.

Informed as I was from a very tender age that eating wild mushrooms involves a certain calculated risk, I thought it prudent to mitigate this danger and ensure my husband was not left bereft as a result of any mushroom misadventure on my part. No, I did not take out life insurance, although the thought did cross my mind. Instead, I sought out insurance of a different kind – an experienced guide. Someone who could navigate a path to the good mushrooms and steer clear of the bad. Someone who had picked and eaten and lived to tell the tale. For that, I turned to two excellent sources of guidance and advice: Gerry

Ivanochko at Saskatchewan Agriculture and Food in La Ronge, and Eugene Bossenmaier, author of a spiral-bound field guide called *Mushrooms of the Boreal Forest*. I made an appointment with Gerry and settled in with Eugene's book for some light reading before bed.

EUGENE'S BOOK is a real page turner, as gripping as any Jane Austen tale of innocent love and doomed romance. It begins with a cautionary tale on page ii, even before the dedication and the table of contents, written in italics so as to emphasize the undeniable truth of the matter: *"If you eat mushrooms you find, you are doing so at your own risk."* As in mushrooms, so in love.

Early on in the story we meet Michael, a burly woodsman living in the boreal forest, who introduces the author to the charms of wild mushrooms. This fateful meeting ignites a passion that consumes the author, who sets off through the forest in pursuit of his new love. As it turns out, this woodsman is a minor character, a bit part, the catalyst who propels the protagonist to action and then steps aside as the story unfolds in an emotional rollercoaster of heartbreak and hope. Michael exits stage left.

Enter *Agaricus*, the genus that includes the lovely button mushrooms we find in the grocery store. This is an encouraging development. But hopes are soon dashed when we learn that the common Woodland Agaricus is easily mistaken for *Amanita virosa*, a mushroom so poisonous it has earned the nickname The Destroying Angel. This angel of death is closely related to another villain, Fly Amanita (which, as the name implies, is toxic to flies), thought to be the orange toadstool that Alice eats in *Wonderland*, creating the hallucinogenic experience of shrinking to a mere six inches tall. Clearly, the wild *Agaricus* is a fellow best avoided.

Turning the page, I come face to face with an image so horrible it makes me shudder, a mushroom that for me epitomizes all the dangers lurking on the forest floor, the *Coprinus comatus*. From the picture, it could be described as having a long cylindrical cap, shaggy and white, with a brown crown and brackish scales. A vile-looking character to be sure. But just as I am prepared to mistrust this fellow forever, I read on and discover that he is quite misunderstood – in fact, he is a good bloke, known as the Lawyer's Wig, and perfectly safe to eat.

Next, we are introduced to his poor second cousin, the Inky Cap. Here, the author skilfully foreshadows Inky's downfall. Unable to stifle my curiosity, I read ahead and learn the sad truth: Inky has a drinking problem. When taken with alcohol, he is prone to induce a rapid heart-beat, ruddy face, tingling in the extremities and nausea. Perhaps a fine fellow for a campfire picnic, but obviously not material for a romantic dinner over a bottle of wine.

As the pages turn, we meet a parade of characters – the delicious Oyster Mushroom and his odoriferous twin, Smelly Oyster, ugly but reliable Pig's Ears, and that charlatan, False Chanterelle. We encounter the gregarious *Gomphidiaceae* family with several dishy offspring but with names like Slimy Pegs and Pine Spikes, perhaps less to my liking than the rugged Man on Horseback or the Train Wrecker. And just when I find myself falling in love with *Morchella elata*, the Black Morel, we encounter his deadly imitator, the False Morel. Rumour has it that an adventurous lover might mitigate the poison of the False Morel by boiling it vigorously in water, but the cook who breathes the fumes may find it to be the kiss of death.

Perhaps the reader will champion the heroic king of the forest, the *Boletus edulis*, a.k.a. the legendary Porcini, cherished among European lovers of mushrooms. But in the end, the author seems to favour the

Hedgehog Mushroom, a steady, reliable character, not overly handsome but fortunate enough not to have an evil twin. They say that nice guys finish last, but in a romance novel, the last page is exactly where you want to be.

MUSHROOMING IS BEST DONE after a good rain, but that summer, rain was a scarce commodity. The forest was tinder dry and, according to news reports, several wild fires the size of Lichtenstein were raging out of control way up north. Now and then, when the fires are bad, the smoke drifts so far south on the prevailing winds that the city of Saskatoon is bathed in the husky scent of *eau de campfire* and the morning sun glows an eerie orange through the haze. But not this morning. It was the dawn of a sparkling August day, bright and blue, with no sign of smoke or rain in the forecast as I stashed the essential paraphernalia of a mushroom picker into my car: ice cream pails, compass, hat, paring knife, several cotton bags, a bear bell, mosquito spray, water bottle, picnic blanket, the mushroom picture book and, last but not least, a friend.

This friend was part of my aforementioned insurance plan. Should I become lost, bitten or poisoned while foraging for mushrooms, he would ensure I did not suffer alone and without succour in the great woods. But above all, he was insurance I would not die of boredom on the long drive to La Ronge. As an avid gardener and forager, my friend David could be counted on as someone who would spend four amicable hours in a car on the promise there *might* be mushrooms at the other end, and remain good humoured on the return trip even if there weren't.

True enough, conversation flowed as effortlessly as the highway, especially after, somewhere north of Prince Albert National Park, the radio signal fizzled and disappeared. There was a flurry of road signs near the park, but beyond we noted little evidence of human activity along the route. No rest stops. No speed traps. No signs advertising "Next gas *waaaay* up ahead." The highway ran wide and empty through the endless evergreens. Occasionally we met a logging truck or a suv hauling a motor boat, and once we were passed by a sleek black car driving at autobahn speeds. I don't recall seeing a sign declaring the speed limit, but if there was one, it was being completely and utterly ignored.

Fortified with coffee and muffins, the drive passed pleasantly enough, and we arrived in La Ronge with time to spare before our one o'clock rendezvous with Gerry. Since neither of us was feeling peckish, we decided against stopping at a restaurant for lunch, opting instead for a picnic in the forest later in the afternoon. And for that, we headed to the Robertson Trading Post for supplies. Old Mr. Robertson began his career as a fur buyer for the Hudson's Bay Company, a connection that David shared: his Scottish great-grandfather operated a Hudson's Bay trading post at the Red Earth First Nation near Carrot River, and his grandfather grew up there, trapping and trading in fluent Cree.

Those who believe that time travel is impossible have never been to Robertson's in La Ronge. Robertson's is one of the last authentic fur trading posts where you can bring in a stack of pelts and leave with a bag of flour or a string of coloured beads. It is also a grocery store, out-fitter, woodsman's haberdashery and a museum of traditional Cree craftwork. The few steps from the front door to the back door are, by my reckoning, the shortest distance between the modern world and the nineteenth century.

We made a beeline past the rack of souvenir t-shirts and coffee mugs, past the Wonder bread and tinned soup, past the oil lamps and camping gear, past the beaded leather jackets and the birch bark canoe, to the back of the store where the walls are hung with trophy fish and photographs, and the paraphernalia of hunting and trapping is sold alongside beaded moccasins, medicine bags, snowshoes and fur-lined gauntlets. The fur-trading counter is nestled in an alcove in the wood-panelled wall, beneath an impressive rack of antlers and a couple of antique guns. In this setting, the dairy cooler looks rather incongruous, all bright white and humming with efficiency, but even it does double duty as a display shelf for hand-carved moose antlers and pretty baskets made of birch bark.

In the midst of this colourful scene, I found my eye drawn to the one item that was starkly black and white: the long, glistening pelt of a grand old skunk. A Cree elder in a buttoned-up plaid shirt was leaning on the counter where the furs are bought and sold.

"That would make a nice coat for you," he said as I stroked the silky fur.

"You think so?" I put the fur to my cheek. There was no hint of the skunk's odoriferous calling card.

"What's this one?" I asked, fingering a luscious brown fur hanging behind the skunk.

"Beaver."

"And this?"

"Otter."

"I like this one best," I said, draping the skunk over my shoulder like a stole. When I was a child, I remember my dad waging a battle with a skunk that had slipped into the pit of the grain elevator on the farm. The slope of the pit was lined with sheet metal, too smooth for the skunk to walk up, so Dad lowered a wooden board into the pit, and when the skunk emerged, he finished it with a shotgun. It was an unfortunate end, but you can't have a skunk poking around a farm with chickens and little kids, both tending to be of the free-range variety. Now I regretted we had not saved the pelt.

"I would scare away all the men with a coat like this, wouldn't I?"

"Not everyone," chuckled the hunter.

"No," said David, "you wouldn't scare away a man with a gun, but that's probably not the kind of attention you were talking about!"

I gave the furs one final hug and turned my attention to our picnic lunch. Being a modern grocery store, Robertson's offered a worldly selection of foodstuffs, and we managed to fill our basket with a mix of Old World and New: muskox salami, caribou jerky, bagels and a couple of bananas. Back in the car, we followed the main road along the shore of Lac La Ronge, a big lake dotted with pretty islands of fir trees. We passed a beach and the marina, where float planes and motorboats come and go, past shops and hotels, past Kosta's and The Zoo (both institutions of nourishment, the latter being nourishment of the liquid kind).

We found Gerry in his office in a sunny, plant-filled government building at the north end of town. At first blush, it seemed a bit incongruous that the ministry of agriculture would station a man smack dab in the middle of a forest, until he explained that his job is to investigate the potential harvest from the forest *other* than the trees. This is the opposite of the expression "can't see the forest for the trees," since it is his job to look right past those trees and see what else of value is lurking on, or near, the forest floor. This includes mushrooms, wild rice, berries, herbs and medicinal plants such as fireweed, an extract of which is soothing sunburns and diaper rash around the world.

Gerry suggested a short tutorial on mushrooms before venturing into the field. While I was anxious to get out and observe the real thing, I had to concede that a little reinforcement of Mr. Bossenmaier's picture book was probably a good idea, given the life-and-death nature of the venture. We learned there are three varieties of mushrooms picked and sold on a commercial basis in northern Saskatchewan: morels, chanterelles and pine mushrooms. Most of these mushrooms leave the country within hours of being picked, destined for markets in Europe, the United States and Japan. The wild mushroom harvest is worth about one million dollars a year to the local economy and, I daresay, considerably more than that by the time it reaches a hungry diner on the other end of a dinner fork.

David and I drew our chairs up to Gerry's computer as he showed us pictures of the edible mushrooms we were likely to encounter that day.

"This is a chanterelle," he said.

I recognized it from the picture book. It was an apricot-orange mushroom with a curvy and somewhat convex cap and, on the underside, long ridges running down a shapely stem. It looked distinctly different from the mushrooms we learn to draw as children, the ones that resemble wide open umbrellas on a stick. (Mr. Bossenmaier's book had cured me of that visual misconception with pictures of mushrooms aptly described as funnel, fan, coral, club, bells, brains and donkey ears.) I had never seen a chanterelle growing in the wild, but I was quite confident that, with the image reinforced on my mind's eye, I could indentify this lovely little darling in an instant. Gerry switched pictures.

"This is the false chanterelle."

We were looking at an apricot-orange mushroom with a curvy and somewhat convex cap and, on the underside, long ridges running down a shapely stem.

"Don't pick this one," he said.

"But they're identical," I protested.

"Not quite," said Gerry. "You can eat one of them. The other one will make you sick."

He proceeded to point out some nuance in the different nature of the ridges on the underside of the cap, one being true ridges and the other being gills. This minor detail did not restore my confidence; in fact, it had the opposite effect. It seemed that every safe mushroom had a dangerous doppelganger. Sensing my flagging spirits, Gerry guaranteed that if and when we saw them up close and personal, we would be able to tell them apart like fraternal twins.

"Don't worry," he assured us. "There are many mushrooms in the forest that will make you sick, but very few of them will kill you."

Next, a picture of three mushrooms in successive stages of growth, like side-by-side photos of a precocious child at the ages of six, nine and twelve. The first was the cutest little button. The middle one was bigger and knobby, its unopened cap still attached to the stalk and bursting at the seam. The third had matured into a full-fledged mushroom with a distinct ring where the rim of the cap had pulled away of the stem. It was the pine mushroom or, in Japan, the prized *matsutake*, which, I have read but scarcely dare to believe, might fetch more than two hundred dollars in a fancy restaurant in Tokyo.

"What does this look like?" asked Gerry, pointing to the littlest mushroom. The cap was no bigger than the tip of a finger, bulging over the top of the stem like a winter toque. If I were a less modest person, and had I made Gerry's acquaintance longer than a mere fifteen minutes ago, I might have set decorum aside and stated that this exuberant little mushroom looked strangely –

"Phallic," said David. "It's distinctly phallic."

"Right," said Gerry. "And that is why it's prized among the Japanese for imparting a manly vitality and good luck."

"Does it work?" asked David.

"Well," said Gerry, "after today, you tell me."

The tutorial over, we followed Gerry's pickup truck from the parking lot and out of La Ronge by the same highway on which we had arrived. A short drive south of town, we turned east onto a dusty logging road that cut a wide swath through the pine trees, looking for all the world as if the forest had been parted like Moses' parting of the Red Sea.

We had not gone far when Gerry caught our attention by tapping his brakes and stretching his arm out the driver's side window. There, in a clearing in the woods, we spied a couple of white tents and a pickup truck. It was the weigh station of a mushroom buyer who had come to scoop up the day's haul from a whole host of pickers and whisk it away to the nearest airport. It seemed a happy arrangement – local folks earn some cash by spending a pleasant day in the forest, and forty-eight hours later, Japanese businessmen stoke their virility for the price of three months' worth of Viagra.

Some way further on, Gerry slowed and steered his truck off the road and down the slope of the ditch. I eased my car over the edge and pulled up behind him. Finally, the moment I had planned for, studied for, salivated for had arrived. I felt the exhilaration of danger, the flush of courage, the high of high-stakes adventure (and not because I had eaten any of *those* kind of mushrooms). I had a date with fate and I was ready for it.

We grabbed our mushroom-picking gear and followed Gerry into the forest, stepping from the sunlight to the cool dim quiet of the pines. The sun filtered through the tops of the trees like gold and made short shadows of fallen logs and undulations in the carpet of moss. I took a deep breath and filled my lungs with the intoxicating aroma of pine and humus. My eyes were still adjusting to the soft light when Gerry stooped to one knee, twisted his knife in the moss and extracted a full-grown pine mushroom. He dropped it into my cotton sack.

"For your husband," he said. He gently pulled apart the moss with his fingers and plucked another, tinier pine mushroom that was hiding underneath. It was a perfect specimen, no longer than my thumb with a snugly worn cap.

"Pine mushrooms grow in clusters. When you find one, you'll probably find more growing under the moss," Gerry explained. "Once they poke through, the cap has probably opened and they're not as valuable to the Japanese. You want to find them young and still under the moss."

This was a curious prospect. Spotting a tiny mushroom in the forest seemed as tricky as spotting a dinghy on the high seas, let alone finding one concealed *under* the moss. I looked around and there wasn't a mushroom to be seen – just endless trees, fallen logs, the green moss, low shrubs and little white butterflies flitting through the sunbeams.

My eye followed a butterfly as it skipped through the woods and landed on a stump. Then a magical thing happened. Not only were my eyes adjusting to the shadows, they were adjusting to the scale, from the macro to the micro, from the forest to the trees to the world at my feet, and suddenly I saw that the forest floor was teeming with mushrooms. Mushrooms in all their glorious variety, growing on trees and tree stumps, on logs and beneath logs and in the moss. Mushrooms that were safe to eat and, no doubt, many that definitely were not.

We fanned out in the forest, walking like troglodytes hunched over with our heads down and our eyes sweeping the ground. Gerry was the first to spot a chanterelle and called us over. It was a cluster of three, looking picture-perfect beside a fallen log. He deftly cut the stems of the larger two with his paring knife but left the smallest one, which was no bigger than a quarter. That, we learned, is mushrooming etiquette – always cut the stem to leave the roots intact and leave the littlest ones for another day.

We spent a pleasant hour or so walking silently in the woods, each of us picking our own path but never quite out of sight of each other. Now and then, a heavy logging truck roared in the distance, but otherwise it was peaceful with the sound of pine needles rustling in the breeze and the crackle of dry twigs underfoot. One by one, a pine mushroom and a chanterelle made its way into my cotton sack.

The sun was on its way west when Gerry called us together to bid his farewell. The tutorial was over and he had to get back to the office. We inspected my haul, which could be more accurately described as a handful. There were no more than a dozen mushrooms in my sack. The makings of one *pasta con funghi*, but hardly enough to keep me in mushrooms for a year of eating locally. I could already see the television commercial for this little adventure:

> Miles: 600
> Gas: $60.00
> Picnic: $12.50
> Unused compass: $5.99
> Mushrooms: Priceless

Well, perhaps not entirely priceless. Granted, I couldn't swipe a credit card in the middle of the forest, but that didn't mean a commercial transaction was out of the question. Had we not observed a venue of commerce in the woods? Surely, one customer was as good as the next. Dollar or yen or euro, it's all currency. Isn't a bird with cash in hand better than two birds with credit? Perhaps the mushroom buyer would take pity on a city gal who said pretty pretty please.

"No, thank you!" said David. "I can't afford to pay Japanese prices for Saskatchewan mushrooms."

Gerry intervened. "Perhaps you don't have to pay Japanese prices," he said. "Skip the buyer and go right to the source. The pickers will be coming out of the forest right about now. Offer them a better price."

And so it was decided that we would attempt to buy mushrooms from a mushroom picker and that Gerry would act as our negotiator to seal the deal. This plan did not exactly contravene the spirit of the venture, since we would be hunting for mushroom pickers instead of the mushrooms themselves. If the goal was to fill my buckets with Saskatchewan mushrooms, it seemed unimportant how they were procured, whether they were *picked* or *picked out*.

We got in our vehicles and headed back toward town, and sure enough, just as Gerry had predicted, we spotted a couple of pickers coming out of the forest with tubs of chanterelles. They were an older couple, wiry thin, with worn leathery faces and easy smiles. With Gerry as our front man, we negotiated to fill four of my ice cream pails with mushrooms for less than the price of a *pasta con funghi* dinner for two, wine excluded.

Just as the deal was done, I felt a spit of rain. We followed Gerry to the highway, tooting the horn as he turned north. We headed south into a brilliant sun-shower, the wipers on high while the sun sparkled on every drop of rain and gleamed on the pavement. We ate our picnic in the comfort of the car, feeling high on mushrooms and already dreaming of dinner.

Over the next few weeks, I cooked chanterelle mushrooms every which way. Pasta sauce, lasagna and ravioli. In a stew, in omelettes and in soup. Marinated mushrooms and mushroom paté. As for the pine mushrooms, I cooked them risotto-style with barley in a dish called orzotto (because *orzo* is Italian for barley, as *riso* is Italian for rice). And yes, it did appear to have an invigorating affect on John. In the days to follow, he hilled the potatoes, cut firewood and swam laps with extraordinary zeal. As for me, I was just happy to be alive. High on mushrooms, you might say.

Several months later, John and I went for dinner at a nice restaurant downtown. Featured on the menu was a dish of pasta with a sauce of wild mushrooms.

"Wild mushrooms," I scoffed. "Wild from where? The wilds of the grocery store? The outback of the Sysco truck? Wild my eye." I shut the menu indignantly. I hadn't fallen for the false chanterelle and I wasn't falling for this.

"It's just an expression," said John.

"No, it's false advertising."

"Order something else, then."

"It's the principle," I said. "They're not wild unless they're picked in the wild. If they're cultivated, they're not wild anymore."

The waiter came to our table.

"I have a question," I said, opening the menu to the pasta page. John gave me that look that says please, please don't embarrass me by making an issue of the mushrooms.

"About this wild mushroom pasta."

"Yes," said the waiter, leaning into the table.

"What kind of wild mushrooms are they?"

"Well, I'm not exactly..."

"And where were they picked?"

He paused. "Would you like me to ask the chef?"

I looked up from the menu. Outside, big snowflakes were falling like cotton balls in the street light. A woman hustled past the window, snowflakes sprinkled on her hat, kicking up little snow drifts with her boots. I remembered that lovely day in August, the day of the sun-shower, when I had gladly succumbed to the instant gratification that money can buy – thank goodness – and where, even in the great boreal forest, "wild" comes in several degrees of separation from the modern world.

I smiled at the waiter. "That's not necessary," I said. "I'll have the steelhead trout."

Perhaps the reader will be looking for the morel of this story, but sadly there is none. Morels were out of season and would have to wait until spring.

## IN THE DARK LIKE MUSHROOMS

SO THERE I WAS, bouncing down a prairie trail in a pickup truck driven by lentil and spice farmer Gary Schweitzer, when he hit the brakes hard.

"Mushrooms," he declared, hopping out of the truck.

I looked around. We were stopped in the middle of two fields, golden as far as the eye could see. No trees, no ditch, no shade, no mushrooms. Gary took a bucket and a screwdriver from the back of the truck, knelt down at the side of the road and started digging. Before long, he had extricated a large white mushroom clinging with soil.

"How on earth did you know that was there?" I asked.

He pointed to another spot on the ground, a small cracked mound in the dry earth. And started digging. "Nobody knows about these mushrooms anymore," he said. "Just me and the old-timers."

Back at the house, we carefully peeled the mushrooms until they were clean, cooked them in butter and ate them. I have never seen them since.

## PASTA WITH CHANTERELLE MUSHROOM SAUCE

In mushroom season, I sauté the chanterelles in a pat of butter until they start to wilt, then freeze them for a winter's day.

Pasta (fettucini or rotini) enough for four servings

SAUCE

| | |
|---|---|
| 1 tbsp | butter |
| 2 tbsp | onion, finely chopped |
| 2 cups | chanterelles, chopped |
| 2 tbsp | port |
| 1 cup | cream |
| | Salt and pepper |

Melt the butter in a saucepan and sauté the onion. Add the mushrooms, fresh or thawed. Simmer until the liquid evaporates. Turn up the heat to medium high. Add the port and let it sizzle off. Turn down the heat and add the cream. Heat through, but don't boil, for about fifteen minutes to thicken. Season with salt and pepper to taste. Serve over cooked pasta. John prefers fettuccini but I like rotini. And since I'm cooking...

# MOREL AND WILD RICE SOUP

Here's the morel of the story: all mushrooms are edible, but some only once!

| | |
|---|---|
| 1 cup | dried morel mushrooms |
| 1 tbsp | canola oil |
| 1 | onion, chopped |
| 2 | carrots, chopped |
| 2 | cloves garlic, minced |
| 1 tsp | *each* dried thyme and sage |
| 1 cup | wild rice |
| 8 cups | beef stock or water |
| | Salt and pepper |

Place the dried mushrooms in a bowl and cover with boiling water. Leave to soften and cool. Drain the mushrooms, reserving the water. Chop the mushrooms and place them in a sieve. Hold the sieve under running water to ensure all the silt is washed out of the morels. Squeeze to remove excess moisture.

Heat the oil in a large pot. Sauté the onion, carrots and garlic until soft. Add the mushrooms and herbs. Stir in the wild rice, coating it well with the oil, and cook until it starts to stick to the pot. Add the beef stock along with the reserved mushroom water, being careful not to add any sediment that may be sitting at the bottom of the bowl. Season with salt and pepper to taste.

Simmer until the wild rice is cooked, about an hour.

# MUSHROOM ORZOTTO

Orzo is Italian for barley. Orzotto is cooked just like the Italian dish called risotto, which is made with rice. In fact, you can take any recipe for risotto and make a perfectly good prairie version with pearl barley. And like risotto, you can't put the lid on and walk away. This dish needs your attention.

| | |
|---|---|
| 2 tbsp | butter |
| ¼ cup | chopped onion |
| 1 | clove garlic, chopped |
| 1 cup | sliced mushrooms |
| 1 | sprig thyme |
| | Salt and pepper to taste |
| 1 tbsp | olive oil or canola oil |
| 1 cup | pearled barley |
| ½ cup | red wine |
| 6–7 cups | water or vegetable stock, simmering |
| ¼ cup | parmesan cheese |
| | Fresh parsley to garnish |

Melt half the butter in a saucepan. Sauté the onion and garlic until soft. Add the mushrooms and leaves of thyme. Season with salt and pepper. Cook until the mushrooms are soft. Remove the mixture to a bowl.

In the saucepan, heat the rest of the butter with the oil. Add the barley, stirring until the grains are shiny and have absorbed the liquid and are just starting to stick to the pan. Add the wine and cook until it has evaporated off.

Add one cup of simmering water or stock, cooking until it is almost absorbed, stirring occasionally so it doesn't burn. Add another cup of liquid and, once again, cook, stirring occasionally, until it is almost absorbed. Continue adding liquid and cooking it down until the grains of barley are creamy and cooked through. After six cups, bite into the barely to determine if it needs a bit more cooking, and if so, add the remaining cup of liquid.

Stir in the mushroom mixture and the cheese. I like to add another nub of butter, but that's up to you. Spoon into a serving dish and sprinkle with chopped parsley. It's a meal on its own, or a nice side dish to pork chops or roast beef.

# 7

## THE MERRY CHERRY

### IF LIFE IS THE PITS, I'M SPITTING AS HARD AS I CAN

MANY THINGS CAN GO WRONG in the course of a day. This particular day, it was a flat tire. Well, it wasn't all the way flat, just visibly low, so I drove to a neighbourhood convenience store to use the air pump. Somehow in the process of hooking the nozzle to the valve on the tire, I managed to let out most of the air that was left. Now it *was* flat. I needed help.

Inside the convenience store, I stood in line next to a glass case containing a heat lamp and a rack of fried chicken parts. At least I think it was chicken, but in truth it was hard to tell what might be inside that thick wrinkled coating. I am sure it was edible, but I'm not so sure it was food. The line was moving slowly and I had time to wonder how we – the vanguard of the twenty-first century – could be so concerned about the state of our health yet so unconcerned about the state of our food.

Ahead of me in the lineup was a good-looking young fellow in a sleeveless T-shirt and a ball cap worn backwards over his curly hair. His arms bulged like melons, obviously the result of sweating under heavy weights. In one hand he had a flagon of carbonated beverage and in the other a fat wallet. He was paying for gas but hesitated just at the moment of swiping his card to ask the clerk for an order of chicken. I had the strange feeling he had read my mind but only got half the message. "Chicken" but not "yuck."

He paid and then it was my turn. I asked the clerk for assistance with the air pump.

"I can't leave the till," he said.

"Is there anyone else?" I asked. He started to ring up the next customer.

"The manager is in the back. You can wait."

Wait was not an option that afternoon. I was on my way to Bruno for the annual Cherry Festival. I had to pick up my friend Tammy and hit the road so we could arrive in time to check into our room before things got underway. That evening we would attend a dinner and Cherry Cheesecake Social. Tomorrow, we would take a tour of the cherry orchard, attend a cherry cooking demonstration, browse the cherry marketplace and sample every item on the menu in the cherry food tent. There were official duties, too. I had been asked to give a little talk about my year of eating locally, during which my husband John and I had fallen head over heels in love with the new Saskatchewan cherry.

In moments like this (i.e., mechanical failure), I call John for help. He finds it hard to believe I once worked in a service station in my hometown, changing oil, patching tires and pumping gas, and I admit it seems as if that teenager in greasy blue jeans was a different person – a younger sister perhaps, but certainly not me. I'll drive out of my way for a full-service gas station so I don't have to hold the pump or wash the windows myself. And I've never changed the oil or a flat on my own car. Come to think of it, going to a convenience store for tire air made as much sense as going there for lunch.

I called my husband from the pay phone, but he wasn't at home. I returned to my car in a rising panic. There, sitting on a bench eating his chicken with great gusto, was the young guy from the store. I felt a pang of guilt for having denigrated his afternoon snack, but I swallowed my guilt like a fish bone and asked him for help. He couldn't have been nicer about it. He wiped his fingers on a wad of paper napkins and tackled my intransigent air nozzle like a pro.

When I finally arrived at her door, Tammy was not the least bit impatient. She kissed her two-year-old goodbye in a flurry of mommy love, grabbed her bag and settled into the car. As we headed out of the city, I related the tale of my misadventure on the way to her house as if it were no more than a comedic interlude. In the face of life's little annoyances, sometimes there is no better option than to laugh and make the best of it. You know what they say: If life gives you lemons, make lemonade. If you're beat, make borscht. If you're in a jam, don't turn to jelly. If life is the pits, *really* the pits, you just might have enough cherries to make a pie. And who doesn't love cherry pie?

As we drove through the countryside, it soon became apparent that no one, aside from the odd human interloper on the highway, was in a hurry for anything. Bachelor buttons waved along the ditches and ducks bobbed in little blue ponds. A farmer hilled his potatoes in a garden beside the road, raising his head and giving a lazy wave as we passed by. The day lost all sense of urgency, which was good, because it was almost suppertime when we pulled into the little town of Bruno and immediately got lost.

It is not easy to get lost in Bruno. It follows the layout of so many small prairie towns – a Railway Avenue perpendicular to a Main Street. All the other streets line up in a perfect grid. Had I followed Railway Avenue to Main Street I would have found our destination, but I was looking for a sign to the Cherry Festival, and finding none, we were soon on our way out the other end of town. I pulled a U-turn.

"Look," said Tammy. "It's Ursuline Street. Take that."

This was a good bit of navigating since the Cherry Festival is held on the grounds of a former Ursuline convent. We parked the car on Main Street just outside the big iron gates and walked through the leafy grounds to the convent, a rambling brick building with a chapel on one end and a gymnasium on the other, evidence of its former service as a residence for the nuns and a boarding school for girls. A big blue-and-white tent had been pitched on the grounds just outside the convent doors, where we were met by a cheerful lady in a prim yellow blouse, beige skirt and sensible shoes. She introduced herself as Sister Maureen, and the little bright-eyed dog in her arms as Sparky.

Sister Maureen explained that she was the only nun still living at the convent, since it was a requirement of the fire insurance that the place be occupied at night. The other nuns had moved away, the school had closed and the building was for sale; a consequence, she said, of the declining number of female students and an even sharper decline in the number who wished to be nuns. However, several rooms had been booked by patrons of the Cherry Festival, so Sister Maureen and Sparky would have some company for the night.

"Does he live here with you?" asked Tammy, cuddling Sparky in her arms.

"Oh, yes," said Sister Maureen. "We're inseparable. You might say" – she smiled coyly – "he's my live-in partner."

The lovely smells of dinner were wafting from the basement hall, and I was reminded that my appetite had recovered from its encounter with the convenience store chicken. We dropped our bags in our room and headed down to dinner in the church hall.

Church dinners are a hearty and satisfying meal. They almost always consist of a big roast of meat (usually turkey or beef), a couple of salads (at least one including cabbage), a pot of potatoes (most often mashed) and fabulous homemade desserts. Church ladies excel at sweets and the prudent diner always saves room for dessert. This evening's menu consisted of roast beef, coleslaw, lettuce salad with raspberry vinaigrette, mashed potatoes with gravy, followed by a Cherry Cheesecake Social in the former chapel upstairs, where Sparky settled down at the ready between our two chairs.

The program that evening included Lois Simmie, who had written a fictionalized account of a real North-West Mounted Policeman who had killed his wife after falling in love with another woman who had no idea her Mountie was already hitched. This was followed by a local poet who had written a poem about her lover licking cherry juice off her naked breasts. The chorus was a salacious "slurp, slurp, slurp" followed by the robust smacking of lips, which the author performed with great gusto before encouraging her audience to join in.

Several stanzas and much slurping later, Tammy noticed that Sparky was no longer sprawled on the floor between our two chairs. No, Sparky had found more promising entertainment under the dessert table, swinging his tail among the stack of empty cheesecake pans and licking with the same enthusiasm as the fellow in the poem. Sister Maureen was nowhere in sight, perhaps having temporarily escaped so much smacking and slurping in the place where she had worshiped for a good many years.

THE CHERRY FESTIVAL did not get underway until eleven o'clock the following morning, so I had arranged to visit the Pulvermacher butcher and grocery store on Main Street. Three generations of Pulvermacher men had been butchers on that spot. Two weeks earlier, they had celebrated one hundred years of the family business, an event that attracted more than three hundred people for a free sausage on a bun.

There is something about the Pulvermacher grocery store that feels more like a cottage than a place of commerce, with its swinging screen door and creaky old floors. The coffee pot behind the meat counter is always on. Just above it is a shelf of mismatched coffee mugs, each one with an owner who washes it out and puts it back after sitting for a spell. There are family photographs on the walls, like the stiff old black-and-white of Alex Pulvermacher, who arrived with a group of German settlers in the early 1900s and set up his butcher shop at the age of twenty-four. The settlers had followed the Benedictine monks, who established a monastery nearby under the leadership of Abbot Bruno Doerfler, the namesake of the town. In the picture, Alex stands in front of a wall of dry goods with an impressive rack of antlers propped on the countertop in front of him.

The Pulvermachers still hunt. Their hunting trophies are mounted on a high shelf, more like the décor of a country lodge than a grocery store – a ruffed grouse over the cereal boxes and a handsome red fox above the household supplies. A large fishing net hangs on the wall over the freezer, dangling with sea shells, fishing lures and other mementoes of scuba diving in exotic climes.

We found Alex's grandson Jerome in his butcher shop, looking the picture of health – fit and tanned, the volunteer fire chief, first responder, hunter, scuba diver, father of three grown children and Mr. July in a calendar of Saskatchewan's Most Eligible Bachelors. The calendar, now set on Mr. August, hung on a pillar near the till. Jerome ran the business with his brother Peter, who was away on vacation.

"When my grandfather opened this store, he couldn't even afford to stock it with groceries," said Jerome. "And here we are, still going one hundred years later."

He explained how his grandfather cut blocks of ice from frozen ponds in winter, put them in an ice box covered with straw and kept the meat cold all summer long. There was a smokehouse out back. Things have changed, of course. Now there is a big walk-in freezer and the smoker is conveniently located in the basement of the store.

"We have electricity now, but other than that, we still do things pretty much the old way," said Jerome. "Everything was handed down, first to my father and then to us. We're lucky enough to stay busy doing things the way they've always been done. I'll never get rich, but it's a good life here in Bruno."

Then he asked one of my favourite questions in the whole world: "Would you like to try something?" Without waiting for an answer, he reached into the glass case and pulled out four different sausages, cut a few thin slices from each one onto a piece of wax paper and set it on his grandfather's butcher's block for us to taste. There was a fat summer sausage, a pale turkey sausage, a robust salami and a brick-red pepperoni stick. The pepperoni was hot with paprika, skinny and rough like it had been stuffed the old-fashioned way by hand. It had barely made acquaintance with my taste buds and I knew this was no ordinary pepperoni. I could tell by the way that Tammy rolled her eyes that her taste buds were sending the same signals as mine.

Jerome wrapped the pepperoni sticks in brown paper, setting the two packages into the meat case to stay cool until our drive home. As we left the store, the screen door swinging shut behind us, I turned to wave goodbye to Jerome, but his eye had been drawn to events in the sky. A grey steamroller of a cloud was bearing down on Bruno, blocking out the sun and chasing up a chilly wind. It had been so lovely that morning that we left the convent without sweaters, and now we wrapped our arms around ourselves and hustled up the street. Despite this sudden turn in the weather, people were streaming through the big iron gates and delicious odours were rising from the circus tent. With breakfast well behind us, and Jerome's sausages to tease our taste buds, it was the perfect moment to slip under the big tent for a spot of lunch.

There was no mistaking the star of this event. The menu board featured cherry pie, cherry sundaes and cherry-topped elephant ears, but the cherry delight that caught my eye was the cherry sausage on a bun. We ordered two and sat down at a round wooden table to eat. A band was warming up the crowd with a jaunty medley of old-time polkas. A small sign leaning on the stage declared them to be Arne's Old Timers – one accordion and three electric guitars. No indication of which one was Arne, but it didn't matter since they were all dressed alike in blue shirts and black pants with big shiny belt buckles.

A section at the back of the tent was cordoned off with a yellow rope and a sign that read: Beverage Section, No Minors Allowed. A smaller sign advertised "Cherry Beverage" for sale. I am a great fan of beverages made with fruit and this cherry sausage on a bun would wash down nicely with a fruity quaff.

"What kind of cherry beverage do you suppose it is?" I asked Tammy.

"Maybe a cherry martini," she said. "Why don't you go find out?"

"It's a bit early, don't you think? It's not even noon."

"It's well past noon in Bavaria." She nodded at the happy fellows in the polka band.

"In that case," I said, "I'll get one for you, too."

I weaved through the tables and past the stage where one of the Old Timers (perhaps it was Arne himself) gave me a hearty wink. Obviously, he was well aware it was happy hour in Bavaria. Alas, no one else had adjusted their watches – the beverage section was empty except for two volunteer bartenders packing cans of beer into a big tub of ice. No martini shaker in sight.

"The Cherry Beverage isn't here yet," said a bartender in a red plaid shirt. "Come back after lunch."

I related the news to Tammy. "Probably a good thing," she said with her nose into the Cherry Festival program, which was printed, appropriately, in red ink. "What time is your talk today?"

"Two o'clock," I said.

"The program says twelve o'clock."

"No, I'm sure they said two."

"But they *wrote* noon."

She slid the program across the table, and sure enough, I was scheduled for noon – which it was, almost. We gulped down the last bites of cherry sausage on a bun and made a quick dash from the food tent up the front steps of the convent. The grey steamroller was now directly overhead and it was spitting a cold rain. This sudden downturn in the weather was unfortunate for the Cherry Festival but a boon for my talk since it could be expected that more people would choose an indoor event over a chilly and waterlogged tour of the cherry orchard. There was a nice little crowd awaiting us in the church hall.

I began my speech on the subject of pies. My husband is a pie man, which is to say, in a choice between cake, cookies, squares, bars (as squares are called where he comes from), strudel, crumble, pudding or pie, he will *always* choose pie. And cherry is one of his favourites. So you can image how delighted we were to discover the new Saskatchewan sour cherry at a U-pick orchard not too far from Saskatoon. In little more than an hour, we had picked enough cherries for a dozen pies.

As we embarked on a year of eating locally, fruit was my biggest concern. Even in the height of summer, it's nigh impossible to buy Saskatchewan-grown fruit in a grocery store. We went to a U-pick for strawberries and apples. A friend invited me to pick his raspberries and another offered his pear tree. I would make my annual expedition to the old O'Hara homestead to pick saskatoons. Nowadays, you can occasionally buy wild blueberries at the Saskatoon Farmers' Market, but back then, you had to stock up at the St. Walburg Wild Blueberry Festival or go up north and pick your own. I picked and froze and canned as much as I could so we would have fruit in our diet even when the temperature outside was thirty below.

As we left that U-pick flush with fresh-picked cherries, I was brimming with confidence that our year of eating locally would not be lacking in fruit. We could forsake imported bananas and oranges and grapes in favour of prairie berries that we picked ourselves. Driving home, I was elated with the success of the venture, until I was struck with a sudden and grievous realization: eight pails of cherries inevitably meant eight pails' worth of cherry pits.

"Man, oh, man," I slapped the steering wheel and groaned, "who's going to pit all these cherries?" Our kitchen gadget drawer is home to a small one-at-a-time pitter that looks somewhat like a syringe with a plunger on a spring. It works marvellously when pitting a few olives for pizza, but enough cherries for a whole pie? It would take days.

"Tell you what," said John. "If you make the pies, I'll pit all the cherries you want."

Now, that's that kind of negotiation that makes for a happy marriage. I accepted his offer before he came to his senses. From this exchange I drew three conclusions: 1) he really *was* into our local diet; 2) he really *did* love cherry best; and 3) he really had *no idea* how many of those little cherries it would take to make a whole cherry pie.

With my official duties over, Tammy and I made our way through the maze of hallways to the convent gymnasium, which had been transformed into the Cherry Marketplace. Vendors were selling their cherry-related wares, from little cherry seedlings to chocolate-covered cherries to cotton aprons in a cheery cherry print. There were other local items for sale, such as birch-twig baskets and beeswax candles and pickled asparagus, but the item that caught my eye was neither natural nor edible. It was a cherry pitter, a deluxe model featuring a chrome plunger, a large capacity hopper for the pits and a suction base that anchored firmly to the countertop. According to the saleslady, it was guaranteed to make cherry pitting as easy as, well, pie.

"I'll take one," I said.

"Sorry," she said. "We're sold out."

My jaw dropped. "Sold out?"

"Yes. They're very popular."

"Can I take this one?" It was the floor model, or in this case, the table model. She declined to part with it.

---

"Come back tomorrow," she said. "We'll have some more."

"But what if I want to make a cherry pie between now and tomorrow?"

She smiled, as if I were kidding. All this talk of pie had put me in the mood for dessert, so Tammy and I made a beeline back to the food tent. I went for a cherry sundae and she indulged a deep-fried elephant ear smothered in cherry sauce. When I finished my sundae I strolled back to the bar.

"About that Cherry Beverage…"

"It's not here yet," said the bartender with a hint of worry in his voice.

"When do you expect it?" I asked.

"Hard to say. It should be here by now." He looked at his watch.

"If you don't mind my asking," I ventured, "what type of Cherry Beverage is it?"

"It's with vodka," he said. "The vodka is already here."

I relayed this information to Tammy. "Maybe a Cherry Paralyzer."

"Or a Bloody Cherry Mary."

"Or a Cherry Wallbanger."

"Or a Red Russian."

We listed off vodka cocktails as we made our way across the convent lawn, through a grove of tall evergreens to the cherry orchard. The steamroller had moved off and the sun was back with considerable force. If ever there was a day to prove that old prairie adage, "if you don't like the weather just wait a few minutes," this was such a day. The orchard tour had just wrapped up and those who had stood through the rain were removing damp jackets and hanging umbrellas over their arms. Even though the rain had stopped, the spitting had not. That is, the cherry pit spitting contest was under way on the far side of the garden.

Let's face it, spitting it not a pretty sight. There are good reasons to denounce spitting in public (it is, in fact, against the law in Saskatoon), and I can't remember ever having spit anything except perhaps a bad nut or a bug that accidentally ran up against the back of my throat. While my husband can spit with considerable force and accuracy, I woefully admit that I spit like a girl. All whiffle and no whomf. Why then, would I subject myself to sure humiliation at the spitting pit? Three little reasons: the only fresh cherries to be had at the Cherry Festival that year were the three ripe cherries doled out to each contestant to extract and spit the pits. All the other available cherries were frozen or processed into something else, since the orchard at the convent was, at that time, still too young to be producing much fruit of its own.

Never too proud to ask for advice in the face of sheer incompetence, I turned to the contestant ahead of me, who was, by happy circumstance, my friend Ramesh, who is a geographer by training with a passable understanding of velocity, gravity and the curvature of the earth. His wife, Karen, perhaps more familiar with the principle of random vectors, was keeping to a safe distance on the sidelines with Tammy and their excitable setter, Mattie.

"You've got to make use of the parabolic velocity and the Coriolis Effect," Ramesh explained. "Like this."

He stretched one foot forward, leaned onto his back leg and arched his back as far as he could without toppling over.

"Now swing forward and, at the top of the arch, release the pit with maximum force."

He demonstrated the technique, spitting his cherry pit a respectable if not record-breaking 5.5 metres or eighteen feet. (The spit to beat was twenty-four feet.) Then he graciously stepped aside and gave me the field. I followed his instructions to a T, leaning back on my right foot, swinging my body forward like a catapult and releasing the cherry pit at the apex of height and speed. It dribbled down my chin.

"You've got it," said Ramesh encouragingly. "You just need to expel the pit with a bit more force. Use those muscles in your cheeks."

My second attempt felt better; I had not quite hit the "sweet spot" but had at least broken the gravitational pull between the cherry pit and my face.

"Five feet," called out the teenager with the tape measure. Not bad, but I could do better. I was down to my last pit. The adrenalin was rising. Ramesh stepped forward to offer a final word of advice.

"How tall are you?" he asked.

"Five-foot-four," I said, popping the third cherry in my mouth and extracting the flesh.

"In that case, you might try a new technique," he said. "Try falling forward, and then spitting just before the moment of impact between your face and the ground. It could be your personal best."

I laughed, of course, but it was a snickering sort of laugh made without opening the mouth because I had a cherry pit in there, and then there was no more cherry pit because I had swallowed it in a snort. In one ignominious moment, my cherry pit spitting aspirations were over and done, choked in my moment of glory.

If I had but a shred of luck left in this unfortunate weekend, I would console myself with a glass of that mysterious elixir, the elusive Cherry Beverage. The four of us walked back to the cherry food tent and, to my great solace, the errant beverage had arrived. It was a syrupy concoction stirred, not shaken, into a shot of vodka. No swizzle stick, no umbrella, no maraschino cherry. But nonetheless, a refreshing consolation to the pit in the pit of my stomach.

ON THE THIRD DAY of the Cherry Festival, the sky was clear as a bell with no rain in the forecast. No flat tire. No tummy ache. No obligations. On the promise of a cherry sausage, a cherry sundae and a Cherry Beverage, I lured John into the car for a return trip to Bruno. However, my primary motivation was even more magnanimous: There was a cherry pitter with his name on it.

We arrived at the orchard just as a tour was getting underway. Our guide was a tall, bearded plant scientist named Bob Bors who gave a history of the cherry breeding program at the University of Saskatchewan and pointed out the different varieties growing there. I was familiar with some of the cherries – the u-pick cherries had been an early cultivar called Carmine Jewel – but the newer cherries had been christened with even more romantic names: Romeo, Juliet, Cupid and Valentine.

"Lovey-dovey names," said the scientist, looking a tad embarrassed by it all.

And why not? Why shouldn't these darling cherries be named for legendary affairs of the heart? They certainly were a labour of love. He related to us the story of the government arborist who began breeding cherries in the 1940s with stock from Siberia. He had been ordered to give up the cherries and focus his efforts on breeding shelterbelt trees, but he could not extinguish his passion. He continued the affair in secret.

"This cherry will be his greatest accomplishment," said Bob, "all because he disobeyed the government."

However, I learned there is another good reason for these love-related names: the colour red. Turns out these cherries are red through and through, unlike the more popular pie-filling cherry, the Montmorency, which is yellow inside and requires a spot of food colouring to make a cherry pie that is truly red. And while these cherries are tart, I was surprised to learn they actually have more sugar content than a sweet Bing cherry. Their tartness comes from a high level of vitamin C.

"Did you hear that, John?" I whispered, wrapping my arm through his. "All my life I thought tart was the opposite of sweet, but now I learn it's possible to be acerbic and sweet at the same time."

"Yes, sweetheart," he said.

When I was a child, my mom had a book by Erma Bombeck called *If life is a bowl of cherries, what am I doing in the pits?* Well, I have an answer for you, Erma. You've got to crack an egg to make an omelette. And you've got to pit cherries to make a cherry pie. On those days when nothing is going right – days full of little annoyances and embarrassing mishaps – on such a day as that, I'm going to get out my deluxe cherry pitter, suction it to the countertop and ask my husband to go make pits.

## RED DINNER

WE RARELY EAT OUT on Valentine's Day. The restaurants are too crowded, the staff is too busy and you can't get too amorous in a public place. So, I cook a local dinner for two at home. To make it extra special, every item I cook is red. This might include a baked ham, tender rare lamb or pasta with red pepper pesto; red-skinned potatoes, a beet salad or red cabbage coleslaw; lingonberry cookies, raspberry mousse or a cherry pie. I have never attempted a colour-coded dinner other than red. Somehow, I don't think another colour would be as fun.

# BEET AND WALNUT SALAD

Now we're really seeing red.

| | |
|---|---|
| 2 | small tender beets, stems untrimmed |
| 1 tbsp | water |
| 1 tbsp | brown sugar |
| ¼ cup | walnuts, chopped |
| | Salad greens for two, including tender beet greens |
| 2 tbsp | goat cheese, crumbled |

DRESSING

| | |
|---|---|
| ½ tbsp | white balsamic vinegar |
| ½ tbsp | fruit syrup (such as chokecherry or raspberry) |
| 3 tbsp | olive or canola oil |
| | Dash of salt |

Cook the beets in boiling water until they are easily pierced with a sharp knife. Cool. Trim the beets, then peel them with your hands under running water. Cut into a bite-sized dice.

Meanwhile, heat the tablespoon of water in a non-stick skillet. Add the brown sugar and stir until dissolved. Add the walnuts, cooking and stirring until the water has evaporated and the sugar has caramelized on the nuts. Cool.

Make the dressing by whisking together the vinegar, fruit syrup, oil and salt. Toss half the dressing with the salad greens and the other half with the beets.

To serve, divide the salad greens onto two plates. Scoop the beets into the centre of the greens. Scatter each with half the walnuts and a sprinkling of cheese.

# LINGONBERRY PASTRY PINWHEELS

One day in summer, I left a cookie on the patio table and a little bird pecked it into a perfect little heart. These cookies, on the other hand, are shaped like hearts...and they're red.

| | |
|---|---|
| 1 half | package of puff pastry, thawed |
| ½ cup | frozen lingonberries (a.k.a. low-bush cranberries) |
| ½ cup | walnut pieces |
| 3 tbsp | brown sugar |
| 1 tbsp | honey |
| | Pinch of grated orange rind |

With a sharp knife, chop the berries and walnuts together until they are well mixed. Stir them into the brown sugar, honey and a small pinch of orange rind. Sample, adding more orange rind to suit your taste.

Roll the pastry into a rectangle roughly 12 x 8 inches. Spread the berry-walnut mixture over the pastry. Roll the long sides of the pastry toward the centre, so that the two rolls meet in the middle. Using a sharp knife, cut the roll into ½-inch slices. Lay the slices on a cookie sheet lined with parchment paper or a silicon mat. Give them plenty of room to expand in the oven. Using your fingers, shape the bottom of each cookie into a point, so they looked like hearts. Bake at 400° F for about 12 minutes.

# PORK TENDERLOIN WITH SOUR CHERRY SAUCE

This is a great dish for a festive occasion because it's made ahead and eaten cold. And it's red.

| | |
|---|---|
| 2 tsp | anise seeds |
| 1 tsp | coarse salt |
| ½ tsp | black peppercorns |
| 1 tsp | dried rosemary |
| 1 | 1-lb (0.5 kilogram) pork tenderloin |
| 2 tbsp | vegetable oil (canola or olive) |
| ½ | medium onion, very thinly sliced |
| 1 | clove garlic, very thinly sliced |
| ½ cup | water |
| 1 cup | frozen sour cherries, thawed |
| ¼ cup | honey |
| 1 tbsp | soy sauce |

In a spice grinder, pulverize the anise seed, salt, peppercorns and rosemary. Rub the pork tenderloin with 1 tbsp of oil, then rub the spice mixture into the meat.

On medium heat, warm the remaining oil in an ovenproof baking dish. Add the pork tenderloin and sear on all sides. Add the onions and garlic and cook until softened. Place the pot, uncovered, in a 400°F oven. Bake until the pork is cooked (when a thermometer pressed into the flesh reads 155°F), about 30 minutes.

Remove the pork from the pot and cool to room temperature, wrap with tinfoil and place it in the fridge for a couple of hours.

Place the pot with the onions over low heat. Add the water and bring to a simmer, scraping up the brown bits on the bottom of the pot. Add the sour cherries and their juice, honey and soy sauce. Simmer, stirring, until the sauce is bubbly and thickened. Mash the cherries with a fork or potato masher to break them down.

Cool the sauce. To serve, slice the cold tenderloin thinly on the diagonal and top with the cherry sauce.

# 8

## IN A PICKLE

### WHEN LOVE GOES SOUR

- - - - - - - - - - - - - - - - - - - - - - - - - - - - - - - - - - - - - - - -

THERE COMES A TIME in the life of every farm family when transition forces a momentous change in the established order of things. Quite often, this change is precipitated by retirement – passing the torch (or the tractor) from one generation to the next. And no matter how we might anticipate such transitions occurring sometime down the road, we are often blindsided by the unanticipated consequences when that day finally arrives.

So it was one blushing spring afternoon on the farm, the lilac buds swelling and mare's tails sweeping the sky, when my mother made a shocking announcement. She and Dad were moving to a house in town so my brother Tom and his family could move from the city to the farm. This was not the shocking news, as the move had been planned for a year. It was the unintended consequences that hit hard.

While I was sad to lose my childhood status in the house where I grew up – the house that still had a pink plaque marked "Amy's Room" on a bedroom door – I was happy to see those sturdy old walls occupied by another generation of children. I had long anticipated this day would come. But for John, the transition was far more devastating for what he hadn't anticipated: the sudden and irrevocable loss of his favourite dill pickles.

Since Mom would be trading her farm garden (large enough to plough with a tractor) for a tiny town garden (barely large enough to turn a rototiller), she would no longer be growing cucumbers. And without cucumbers, there would be no more homemade pickles. As if to cement her decision, she gave John a big jar of dill pickles stuck with a hand-written note: Last jar of pickles 2005.

For John, it had been love at first bite. He declared them to be the best dill pickles he had ever crunched alongside a bratwurst or sliced into a ham sandwich. Mom gave him jars of pickles as gifts, which he rationed between birthdays and Christmases so as never to run out. He felt like a rich man if there was more than one jar of Mom's pickles in the house. And so he was more than a little woebegone at this unexpected turn of events.

"Do you think she meant it?" he asked on the drive back to the city.

"Sounds like it."

"What are we going to do?"

"Do? What can we do? Force my mom to make pickles at the point of a pitchfork?"

He had already considered several options:

Plan A: I would grow cucumbers and take them to Mom for pickling.

Plan B: I would buy cucumbers and take them to Mom for pickling.

Plan C: I would learn to make pickles at my mother's side. This final option was least attractive to me because I don't particularly like dill pickles. In this, I am my mother's daughter. In more than four decades of making pickles, she has never eaten a single one, and neither have I.

"How about Plan D," I said. "YOU grow, buy or make the pickles yourself."

I tried to imagine my mother having this same conversation with her new husband forty-odd years ago. She was a city girl who had never learned to cook (although her mother was a great cook), who had married right out of university and moved directly from her childhood home to the big house on the farm.

"But honey," she said to Dad in my imagination, "I don't like dill pickles."

"But sweetheart, I do."

"But can't we just buy them?"

"And let all these cucumbers go to waste?"

Waste not, want not, and Dad wanted pickles. Fortunately, Mom's new mother-in-law was living with them on the farm and she taught Mom everything she needed to know in the kitchen, including how to make pickles. No doubt Grandma had learned to make pickles from her mother or perhaps her older sister Lizzie. In turn, she taught her own daughters, and so it was the most natural thing in the world to teach her daughter-in-law, too.

Once I began to see pickles for what they really were – not just a jar of sour cucumbers but a cultural continuum through a long line of female ancestors dating all the way back to the Old Country – I began to wonder why Mom had not yet taught me to make them.

"Mom," I asked over the telephone, "why didn't you ever teach me how to make pickles?"

"But you don't even like pickles."

"True," I said, "but it's tradition. And you've spoiled my husband and now he doesn't want any dill pickles but yours."

And so, one evening in August, I loaded my car with cucumbers and headed to Mom's new kitchen in Craik. I had purchased the cucumbers in the city that day, at a farmers' market in the parking lot of a shopping mall next to a fleet of seniors' condominiums. As I stood in line with a bag of cukes under my arm, a silver-haired grandmother nudged me from behind.

"Don't forget the dill," she said. "You'll need lots of dill."

Dill grows like a weed in my garden, but I grabbed a big bouquet of dill and she nodded at me approvingly.

"And garlic," she said, as if warning me against a fate that only garlic could dispel.

My mom is to garlic as Winston Churchill was to vermouth. (He was said to merely glance at the bottle of vermouth whilst making his martini.) For my mom, the mere presence of garlic in the room was quite garlicky enough. In other words, I didn't need extra garlic. But I felt it was a good omen that this grandmother had offered her advice, and I could always use the garlic in something else.

Early the next morning, we got down to work. Mom sterilized the jars by dousing them in boiling water. My sister Maureen peeled the garlic (yes, one small clove per jar). I scrubbed the cucumbers and laid them out according to size – small, medium and biggish. Outside the kitchen window, the morning was a dewy green and the flag hung perfectly limp, wrapped around its pole. As we worked, Mom talked about her first year on the farm. She was just twenty years old, less than half my current age, and knew little more about baking than how to crack an egg.

"I was as green as grass on the prairie," she said. "When Grandma Ehman asked me to make an angel food cake, I said, sure, where's the box?"

"Box?" laughed Grandma. "The chickens lay eggs all day and you want to make an angel food cake from a box?"

Mom learned then and there to make an angel food cake from scratch with the whites of a dozen eggs. And years later, she taught her two daughters to make an angel food cake from scratch. Just recently, Maureen took an angel food cake to her in-laws for dinner; a cake, she admitted, made from a box.

"They were mightily impressed," she said. "Impressed that I had baked a cake in my own oven – who cares about the box – because they usually buy their angel food cakes ready-made from the grocery store."

So, you see, there's scratch baking and there's scratch-scratch baking, and while I am not the least bit reluctant to take advantage of a modern convenience in the kitchen, it is nice to know how to do things the way that Grandma did.

As we made our way through each step in the pickle assembly line, Mom prefaced her instructions with: "That's the way Grandma did it." It seemed that in four decades of pickle-making nothing had changed, not even the water. The water on the farm comes from a dugout that fills in the spring and, in my humble opinion, tastes nothing short of horrible. If it were a glass of wine I would describe it as having an

---

earthy nose, a bitter palate and a mineral finish that lingers far too long. But maybe, just maybe, that farm water was the key ingredient that made my mom's pickles snap to attention like an eager Boy Scout.

Of course, Mom had thought of that, too, and there on the counter was a big blue jug of tap water from the farm. While I might refuse to drink it straight up in a glass, this was serious pickle business, and I saw no reason to tinker with tradition. We measured twelve cups of farm water, two cups of vinegar and ¾ cups of coarse salt into a pot and set it to boil on the stove. Unlike many recipes for dill pickles, Mom's uses no pickling spice of any kind. I dropped a tiny clove of garlic and three big sprigs of dill into each jar and began packing under her watchful eye. First the bigger cucumbers formed a circle inside the glass. Then a few middle-sized cucumbers were pressed into the gaps. And finally, using a thumb and thirty pounds of pressure, the smallest cucumbers were squeaked into the slightest remaining space.

Once the jars were stuffed with cucumbers, I poured in the hot brine, applied the rubber seals and twisted on the lids. Then we turned the jars upside down on a piece of newspaper. This was Grandma's method of testing whether the seals were tight. If the paper became damp under a jar, it was opened, wiped clean and the lids reapplied. Once all the seals were tight and dry, I packed the pickles into a box, put it into the back of my car and drove out to my brother's farm for lunch.

The day was hot and still. Up ahead, a fleet of little clouds crossed the sky like an armada heading south. The gravel road ran straight as an arrow as far as the eye could see and each passing vehicle raised a plume of dust that hung over the road like a veil. I gave the country wave, lifting two fingers of the hand at the top of the steering wheel, and every driver waved back.

I turned on the car radio and by marvelous coincidence, the

Bernardin lady was talking about home canning. Bernardin is the company that makes jars and lids and other supplies for canning. The Bernardin lady was taking calls and answering questions from listeners, and she was contradicting just about everything I had just learned about making pickles.

You should use soft water. Did we? No.

You must boil the empty jars to sterilize them. Did we? No.

You must boil the filled jars to seal them. Did we? No.

You must leave the jars undisturbed on the counter for twenty-four hours.

"Modern science has taught us a few things about food safety," scolded Ms. Bernardin. "We no longer do things the way our grandmothers did."

As I bounced down the country road, my newly minted jars of pickles tinkling together merrily in the back of the car, I scoffed at Ms. Bernardin. Curse this modern inclination to reject the past as old-fashioned and unsafe. Grandma never killed anyone with her pickles. Nor her mother before that. What do we know from our test kitchens and food science that generations of women didn't figure out long ago? Who needs a food scientist to tell us how to make pickles when Mom is there to teach us?

A week later I called my mom in a panic. An odd white powder had settled onto my pickles like the flakes in a snow globe. She was having the ladies for tea and I could hear their chatter through the telephone.

"That's never happened to me," she said. "Let's ask the experts."

The conversation subsided momentarily as she posed the question. Then it resumed enthusiastically, debating the merits of hot pack versus cold pack, boiling jars versus baking jars, water bath versus pressure cooker, right side up versus upside down. When Mom came back on the phone she had sifted through a collective 350 years of pickle wisdom and had synthesized the very best advice.

"Pour out the brine, wash the jars and start over."

"But what about the farm water?" I said. "I need farm water for the brine."

"Oh, *really*," she said. "Water is water."

I sat down at my kitchen table in a state of confusion. Perhaps I had been too eager to make my mom's pickles. Was I competing with her for the pickle affection of my husband? Why take that away from a mother-in-law? Why erase that memory, decades from now, when we're sitting down to a limp dill pickle in the nursing home and John turns to me and says, "I miss your mom's pickles." I might even cry.

No, if I insist on making dill pickles, I should make a pickle so different from my mom's that comparisons are impossible. Eaten side by side in a blind taste test, there should be no confusion about which is which. My poor husband should not be forced to choose one over the other. He should split his affections equally. Mom's pickles would be simple and pure. Mine would be saucy and spicier. I would take my grandmother's pickle and make it my own.

A SHORT TIME LATER, I was travelling the "spice road" in search of ingredients for pickling spice. It was the cool of the morning before a blistering day, when the air is fresh and fills the lungs like silk. The sky was a pretty pale blue over a golden land, just such a morning to imagine a camel caravan departing with its precious cargo for another long walk across the Arabian desert en route to the ports of Alexandria and Venice, where spices were mysterious and worth their weight in gold.

But hey, that's no camel grazing in the pond of a green oasis, it's Bullwinkle the moose. He raised his heavy head and watched my car flash by on the deserted highway. Of course, it wasn't *the* Bullwinkle of cartoon fame, but Bullwinkle was the first moose I encountered as a child and is, therefore, every moose to me. Growing up on the farm, we would no more expect to see a real moose than a real roadrunner or a real Tasmanian devil, but all these years later the moose are migrating south from the forest onto the plain, no doubt in search of food. In the rear-view mirror, I watched him trot across the highway, his head held high as if he could already smell the next watering hole in the distance. This spice road was no ancient caravan trail, but a well-worn blacktop deep into the heart of prairie farmland, the highway that leads to the town of Eston, which is, in my books, the unofficial Spice Capital of Canada. No store-bought pickling spice would do for me. Since my husband and I had embarked on a year of eating locally, we had endeavoured to source all our food in Saskatchewan, whenever possible, and there was no way on God's green earth I was going to compromise on pickles. The pioneers grew cucumbers and garlic and dill; the modern farmer is growing pickling spice, too.

By late morning, I was riding high in the cab of a combine circling a field of coriander, the air filled with an exotic lemony scent. At the wheel was Gary Schweitzer, looking just the typical farmer in blue jeans, a golf shirt and a ball cap. But beneath that ordinary exterior is the heart of a true entrepreneur. In less than two decades, Gary had transformed his wheat farm into a hub of spice production.

This is a strange fate for a kid who grew up swearing he would do anything but farm. He went to university, got a job, had a boss, disliked his job and his boss, and came to the conclusion that farming was one of the few jobs that offered complete independence of mind and spirit. The trouble was, the price for wheat in the 1980s was barely above subsistence wages. He had two choices: get out of farming or farm something else.

What he did next could be described as an act of pure desperation, pure genius, or both. He planted a dozen different seeds that were better known in places like Turkey and Syria and India – things like coriander, cumin, caraway, anise seed, fenugreek, lentils and chickpeas – and waited to see which would grow.

"I planted about twelve rows of individual things with the hope that one of them would grow well here," said Gary. "Darn if ten of them didn't grow. It opened my eyes to the fact that darn near everything grows well here, so what do we do now?"

Well, he did what he does best. He planted those seeds in his fields and reaped the harvest. And then the real work began. He tried to find a marketing company to sell his exotic harvest, but they weren't interested. Who could blame them – they weren't familiar with these seeds and didn't have the buyers. He called the spice companies directly, but that was equally frustrating because they thought he was a kook. According to Gary, the conversation went something like this:

"I'm growing coriander in Saskatchewan."

"You can't grow coriander in Saskatchewan."

"But I am."

"Then it's no good."

"But you haven't seen it."

"Don't need to. Don't call again."

After a couple of harvests, his grain bins were full of exotic crops and he wasn't giving up. He called the spice companies and asked who supplied them. If the product came from Turkey, then who brought it to North America? Who made the big deals? Who could open the door to the new kid on the block? Eventually, a spice merchant in New York agreed to take a look. He liked what he saw, and Gary was in business.

"The spice trade has been around for thousands of years, and trading patterns are so ingrained, there were very few spice traders willing to take a chance on a Canadian farmer," Gary told me. "But when they looked at our product, it was higher quality and lower cost. We're honest, we speak English and when we make a contract we stick with it. Then they asked, if you can do coriander, what else can you do? Can you do caraway, fenugreek, anise seed, dill? And we started to expand the list."

As you might imagine, a strange new plant growing on hundreds of acres in rural Saskatchewan is bound to attract attention. Other farmers got wind of Gary's new venture and asked if they could get in on it. He set up a marketing company to sell his harvest, and offered to sell theirs, too. Today, he markets twenty to twenty-five different crops on behalf of 150 farmers to companies around the globe. Many more farmers have followed his lead – much of the cumin, coriander, caraway, fenugreek, anise seed and mustard seed used in North America is grown in Saskatchewan.

"They said it couldn't be done, but we've proved them wrong," said Gary. "We're a small player in the world spice market, but in North America we're the biggest."

Back at the house, his wife Susanne moved a pile of cookbooks off a chair so I could sit and visit. She cooks dinner every evening for the farmhands, and the meals are especially hearty during harvest time when the workday can last well past sunset. She set a table for them in the cool basement and I carried down a big, steaming spaghetti pie.

Outside, a transport truck rumbled down the driveway. Gary doesn't sell his harvest in quantities smaller than forty-thousand pounds (the equivalent of eighteen-hundred big sacks of flour), which pretty much cuts out me and my little homemade pickle venture. But before I left for home, he slipped me a care package of spices and other goodies from his farm, which I carefully nestled beside me on the front seat of the car.

Somewhere on the highway back to the city, I passed an armoured truck with its hood up at the side of the road and I pulled over to offer assistance. "Everything's fine," said the guy with a gun on his hip. "We've placed a call." He was all business. I would have liked to offer him a ride; to drive down the highway with him riding "shotgun" just to prove that my cargo of spices is still as valuable as gold.

ONE DAY SEVERAL MONTHS LATER, John opened a jar of pickles that startled his taste buds. "These are *not* your mom's pickles," he said, sucking air over his burning tongue. Indeed they were not. My pickles included a pickling spice of Saskatchewan coriander, caraway, anise seed, mustard and fenugreek, fat cloves of garlic, lots of fresh dill and a couple of hot banana peppers from my garden.

"Do you like them?" I asked.

"They certainly are different."

"Good different? Or bad different?"

He took another bite.

"Good different," he said. "Hot and spicy, just like you."

Now, there's another memory for the old folks' home. But this story doesn't end there. The next year, my mom gave John a jar of pickles marked 2006.

"Mom," I said, "I thought you weren't going to make any more pickles."

"I never said that."

"Yes you did. Why else would I learn how to make pickles?"

"Because it's tradition," she said. "I won't be making pickles forever, you know."

## PASS THE SALT AND PEPPER

"WHAT ABOUT…?" How often did I hear *that* during our year of eating locally? What about oranges? What about chocolate? What about salt and pepper? When it comes to salt and pepper, the answer is easy.

I buy peppercorns at the Saskatoon Farmers' Market. The vendor grows pepper on her farm in Costa Rica and brings it back in her suitcase. Sure, it's not grown in Saskatchewan, but it's grown with Saskatchewan hands. Given that it's hard to go without pepper, that one degree of separation is good enough for me. As for salt, I use Saskatchewan sea salt.

Okay, we all know Saskatchewan is far from the sea as the crow flies. But it's less than a mile from the sea *straight down*. A 350-million-year-old dried up seabed. At the Sifto salt mine near Unity, the ancient sea salt is pumped to the surface, dried and packaged as table, rock, kosher, water softener, livestock and icy road salt.

So here's to Saskatchewan's Paleozoic sea salt!

# SALT OF THE EARTH TROUT

I often make this with steelhead trout from Lake Diefenbaker, but it's also a great way to cook northern pike because the flesh lifts neatly off those pesky bones.

| | |
|---|---|
| 1 | 5-lb (2.3-kg) trout or northern pike, cleaned |
| 1 | lemon, sliced |
| 3 | sprigs fresh thyme |
| 1 | 3-lb box coarse salt |

You will need a baking dish that is not much wider than the fish. If the fish is longer than the dish, cut off the head and/or tail to make it fit. Otherwise, leave them on, unless you're like my friend Heather who can't stand to eat something that's staring up at her.

Place the fish in the baking dish. Fill the cavity with lemon slices and sprigs of thyme. Pour on the salt, covering the fish until it entirely disappears. Bake 1 ½ hours at 325°F. If the fish is smaller than 5 lb, cook for proportionately less time.

When it comes out of the oven, the salt will be baked hard. Crack it with a sharp knife. Peel off the salt along with the skin of the fish, then lift the flesh off the bones. For a nice meal, serve with a Wild Rice and Dried Cherry Salad and for dessert, a berry meringue.

# WILD RICE AND DRIED CHERRY SALAD

SALAD

| | |
|---|---|
| 3 cups | cooked wild rice |
| 1 cup | dried sour cherries |
| 2 cups | small broccoli florets |
| 2 cups | small cauliflower florets |
| 3 | green onions, finely chopped |
| ¼ cup | sliced almonds |

VINAIGRETTE

| | |
|---|---|
| 3 tbsp | canola oil |
| 2 tbsp | red wine vinegar |
| 1 tbsp | fruit syrup (such as raspberry or chokecherry) |
| | Dash of salt |

Mix together all the salad ingredients. Put the vinaigrette ingredients into a jar, shut the lid and give it a good shake. Toss the vinaigrette into the salad well ahead of serving so the flavours have time to sink in.

# MERINGUES WITH FRESH BERRIES

MERINGUE

| | |
|---|---|
| 4 | large egg whites at room temperature |
| 1 cup | icing sugar |
| 1 tsp | cream of tartar |
| 1 tsp | vanilla |

BERRIES

Fresh berries, about ½ cup per person
Sugar to taste

VANILLA CREAM

| | |
|---|---|
| 1½ cups | whipping cream |
| 1 tsp | vanilla |

To make the meringue, beat the egg whites on medium speed until soft peaks form. Turn the mixer on high. Add the icing sugar one spoonful at a time, beating well after each addition. When the whites are stiff, sprinkle in the cream of tartar and vanilla and mix well.

Heat the oven to 225°F. Line a baking sheet with wax or parchment paper. Scoop the meringue into six mounds, using the spoon to form circles with a depression in the centre. Bake for about one hour (longer if it's a humid day). When cooked, the meringue will be light and dry; a toothpick inserted in the centre should come out clean. Turn off the heat and leave the meringues in the oven with the door ajar for at least an hour. Store in an airtight container.

Mix the fresh berries with sugar to your taste. You can do this ahead of time so the berries get juicy. Whip the cream with the vanilla. Just before serving, spread whipped cream onto each meringue and top with berries.

# 9
## HOT STUFF
### PASS THE HONEY MUSTARD, HONEY

------------------------------------------------

MY HUSBAND AND I are not very romantic when it comes to giving gifts to each other. I think the most romantic gift I ever gave him was a pair of bright green boxer shorts with little snowmen wrapped in red scarves. He gave me a silver champagne bucket, which is very romantic except that we don't use it often, at least not when it's just the two of us. The truth is, he didn't sweep me off my feet with little romantic gestures, and I didn't charm him with sweetness and candlelight.

However, he does know my soft spot. And it's not for fancy gifts of jewellery or flowers or surprise

------

vacations. The most perfect gift he ever gave me came in a brown paper bag, without a card or a note of any kind, with no return receipt because it didn't cost a red cent.

It was my birthday, less than a month after we had pledged to eat locally for a year and so, as you might guess, my soft spot was a little bit lower than my heart.

"I've got something you really, really want," he teased me.

"Is it food?" I asked, honing in quickly.

"Yes."

"Is it homemade?"

"Yes."

"Is it yellow?"

"Yes."

My taste buds were tingling. I knew I was getting close.

"Is it...Penny's mustard?"

With a flourish, he opened the paper bag, pulled out a big jar of mustard and plunked it into my eager hands. I hugged it to my heart and then, not forgetting the bearer of the gift, gave him a hug, too. Penny's homemade mustard is the best mustard on the planet. It is the colour of...well, mustard, with little red flecks, smooth, not grainy, the consistency of soft honey with a hint of heat. A mere hot dog does not do it justice. It cries out for a slice of sun-warmed tomato on a crisp baguette, or a shave of ham and fresh lettuce on rye, or a juicy bison burger seared over a hot grill.

I have always loved mustard. Growing up on the farm, my favourite after-school snack was a bologna and mustard sandwich – two slices of bologna held together by a sloppy layer of French's mustard. Nowadays, the door of my fridge is spilling over with jars, tubes and squeeze bottles of every sort, from sweet honey mustard to hot horseradish mustard to French Dijon. You might say I'm as keen as mustard about mustard.

However, I am somewhat embarrassed to confess that as a child I made no connection between the yellow mustard on that bologna "sandwich" and those little yellow seeds my dad carted off the farm by the truckload. To be sure, they were both called mustard, but I thought they were homonyms in the same way that *relish* denotes both a condiment and a great delight in something, and *produce* is both a verb and the vegetable section in the grocery store. I relished mustard, but I didn't realize my dad was producing the raw material.

The fact is, Saskatchewan is one of the world's leading producers of mustard seed – yellow seed for good old hot dog mustard, brown seed for spicier European mustards and hot oriental mustard seed, which is crushed to make cooking oils for Asian cuisine. This mustard supremacy dates to the 1950s, in the wake of the Second World War, when the mustard fields of Europe were laid waste by the battle. Who could imagine a German bratwurst without grainy mustard or a vinaigrette without French Dijon? New supplies were required. Turns out, the hot, dry climate of Saskatchewan is perfect for producing mustard with a wallop of heat. My dad grew yellow mustard seed for the food companies that provide us with the classic hot dog mustard, which had pleased my palate from an early age.

Several years ago, John and I were driving though the Wisconsin countryside between Mineral Point and Madison when I spied something by the side of the highway that turned my brake foot to lead. It was a sign for the Mount Horeb Mustard Museum. Now, I would hardly blink at a sign for a ketchup museum, and a relish museum would leave me cold, but a mustard museum was a different cup of condiment. I love mustard. I could not *not* stop.

We were greeted at the door by the Grand Poupon himself, the curator of the mustard museum, who had amassed a collection of more than five thousand mustards from around the world. They lined the shelves of his museum like wallpaper.

"Where are you folks from?" he asked.

"I grew up in Darlington, in southwest Wisconsin," said John, "but we live in Saskatoon, Saskatchewan."

I could tell by the glint in the curator's eye that he wasn't going to ask, "And where is that?" No, he knew his mustard map. For good measure I added: "My dad's a mustard farmer."

His eyes lit up. "Well, let me shake your hand," he said, giving me the kind of handshake reserved for someone you always wanted to meet and finally did. "We don't get many folks from Saskatchewan. Come on in and make yourselves at home." He ushered us in like royalty and sat us down in the Mustard Piece Theater for a private screening (as we were the only visitors there that day) of a short flick on the popularity of mustard around the world.

"He was awfully friendly," said John after the mustard curator had left us alone.

"That's because Saskatchewan is the top supplier of mustard seed in the world. Just about every jar of mustard in here, from French's to Dijon to Keene's, could have a little bit of Saskatchewan in it."

"Well," said John, "that explains it."

"Explains what?"

"Why I feel like I've been here before. It's Dijon vu."

"Too bad you can't mustard a better joke than that," I said.

"I'll have to go a long way to ketchup with you."

"I don't relish the thought..."

AFTER MY FIRST JAR of Penny's mustard, I could love no other. All other mustards were mere dalliances, a little heat on the side, pale in comparison to my main squeeze. As I scraped the bottom of that first jar, I felt as melancholy as if I were saying goodbye to a summer love. Will you ever touch my lips again? Shall I close my eyes and smell you near me, and long for you with every tomato sandwich and sausage on a bun?

Faced with that prospect, I decided that the best course of action was to ask Penny for the recipe for her homemade mustard so I could keep myself in the condiment to which I was accustomed.

"It's easy," she said. "You just..."

"Ahem," interrupted her husband Rick. "That mustard is a secret family recipe, and you're not family."

I suppose if I'd had a son I could have betrothed him to one of Rick and Penny's daughters – marriages have been arranged over lesser treasures. But alas, a mustard alliance between our two families was not to be. Blackmail was out of the question. A ransom note was impractical. I could hold them at knife point – but all I really wanted on my knife was Penny's mustard.

"Okay," I said, "but if you're planning to go into business with that secret family recipe then do it quickly, because I have a habit to feed."

As soon as I said that, I realized how spoiled I'd become. Grocery stores are better than drug dealers when it comes to instant gratification. Supermarkets have wiped out all semblance of the seasons and eliminated the act of longing from our food vocabulary. When we want it, we buy it. We think nothing of eating asparagus in winter and raspberries in spring. In fact, we're upset if we *can't* have them whenever the fancy strikes. Just imagine how much better those raspberries would taste if we awaited their natural season with the same giddy anticipation as a child awaiting Christmas or a special birthday gift. Would Penny's mustard seem less special if I *never* ran out?

I decided to take the Zen approach, free my heart of longing and let desire melt away like Coleman's mustard in a Welsh rarebit. I would treat all mustards with respect, appreciating their unique qualities, like Dijon in a homemade mayonnaise, or honey mustard on a baked ham, or warm potato salad with a grainy mustard vinaigrette. In this unjudgemental state, I might even revisit the bologna-and-yellow-mustard sandwich of my youth. At some enlightened moment, when I was least expecting it, Penny's mustard would come to me. That was mustard karma.

THE ADVERTISEMENT for the Humboldt Oktoberfest caught my eye not for the polka band or the beer barrel rolling contest or the locally made sausage fest (although that did sound good), but for the home-made mustard contest. As much as I have always loved mustard, and grew up surrounded by fields of mustard, and keep my refrigerator stocked with mustard, I had never attempted to make a jar of mustard myself. This was a serious gap in my list of things to do before I kicked the bucket and, while I am not the competitive type, a deadline such as this was exactly the motivation I needed to tick this off my Bucket List.

The date for the Humboldt Oktoberfest was fast approaching. There was little time for experimentation, but how hard could it be? Didn't Penny say it was easy? Of course, I wouldn't have *her* recipe, but surely I could find a recipe just like it on the Internet. On second thought, I wouldn't try to duplicate Penny's mustard. I would make my own signature mustard, a dark and grainy mustard made with that one special ingredient that Penny did not have: mustard seed from my own family farm. I searched the Internet for appropriate recipes, borrowed from this one and that one, and put together a version that was sure to please a vat of German *wurst*.

"Try it," I told John. He stuck his nose in the jar of fresh-made mustard.

"Whoa – how much vinegar did you use?"

"What the recipe called for."

"Whose recipe?"

"Mine," I said proudly.

"Five thousand mustards in the world and you have to reinvent the wheel..."

Of course, I did not expect complete success on the first attempt. Mustard, like anything, requires patience and practice. For my second attempt, I used less vinegar and more wine. On the third attempt, I replaced the wine with beer. For the fourth, a bit of brown sugar. And after four batches of what amounted to so much wasted mustard seed, I had to admit: I couldn't make mustard if my life depended on it.

"I give up," I said to John. "Too bad I can't enter Penny's mustard in the contest."

As soon as I said it, I knew it was a good idea. If Penny makes the best mustard in the world, why shouldn't she reap the rewards? Why shouldn't she be the belle of the Humboldt Oktoberfest, with her mustard splashed across the front page of the *Humboldt Journal?* Perhaps she would be so grateful to the instigator of such good fortune that she would bestow another jar – no, make that two jars – of her homemade mustard on the dear, thoughtful friend who had made this dream come true. This last act was essential to the scenario, since I would have to sacrifice my only jar of Penny's mustard to enter the contest. It was a stiff price to pay.

Driving out to Humboldt that chilly October evening, Penny's mustard nestled in my lap, I felt assured of at least four votes. We had invited our good friends, Heather and Murray, to join us, and since the mustard contest is a People's Choice Award, I was priming them to make the right choice.

"I have no intention of telling you how to vote," I began, "but just look at this jar of mustard." I held up Penny's mustard to be viewed in the last fading light of day. "Look at the colour, that turmeric-yellow with the tiniest flecks of red. Note the smooth, thick consistency."

I tipped the jar to prove it wasn't thin and runny. Murray, who was driving, gave it the scrutiny of a judge through the rear-view mirror. Back then, he was not yet a judge, but a lawyer with a reputation for taking an even-handed and fair-minded approach.

"When you see this mustard on the judging table," I said, my voice rising with passion, "just promise me you'll give it a fair and honest assessment. And if it wins, maybe, just maybe, I can finagle a jar of Penny's mustard for you, too."

"Would that be a bribe?" asked Murray.

"Call it what you like," I said, "but I prefer to think of it as spreading the largess among my loyal friends."

We arrived at the hall in Humboldt just as the festivities were getting underway. On the stage, local fellows in green shirts and alpine hats were warming up the crowd with the Beer Barrel Polka, snapping out that ONE-two-three polka beat that swells the heart of every ethnic Swiss or German. I learned to polka when I was very young by standing on my dad's feet as he ONE-two-three'd around the living room. Unfortunately, this technique was not employable with my new husband, my feet being considerably smaller than his. How could anyone who grew up near Cuca Records of Sauk City, Wisconsin, home of such old-time polka masters as Whoopee Norm Edlebeck and his Dairyland Dutchmen and Syl Liebl's Jolly Swiss Boys, be so inept at the polka?

Well, we hadn't come to Humboldt to dance. We settled into a table at the back of the hall, and while I slipped away to register my entry in the homemade mustard contest, the others sidled up to the kitchen counter for a plate of sausage, sauerkraut, potato salad, *apfelkuchen* and a beer.

The marshals of the mustard contest introduced themselves as Anne and Joe, sister and brother, and by their age I might have guessed their polka days were over. Several jars of mustard were already sitting on the table in front of them. I set Penny's mustard on the table, cleared my throat and launched into a little speech I had composed on the drive.

"I would like to confess up front that I did not make this mustard myself," I said, quickly adding a more fulsome explanation. "My friend Penny made it, and she wanted to be here, but she couldn't come, so I offered to enter her mustard for her."

It was just a small white lie. Anne folded her long, pale hands on the table and looked at me. Joe was silent, as if waiting for Anne to rule on this irregularity.

"It's very good mustard," I said. "It could be a winner."

I was beginning to think I might have to call on my lawyer to argue the case, but then Joe winked and Anne handed me the registration form and I was in. After filling in my personal information, Anne took the paper and carefully read my name.

"I knew your grandmother in Saskatoon," she said. (Grandma was rather proud of me back when I was a television news reporter and had, no doubt, mentioned me to the church ladies.) "She gave me a recipe for hermits."

Grandma Jo (short for Josephine) O'Hara was a consummate collector of recipes. And for every one she received, I'm sure she gave two away. I can remember her writing out recipes in her lovely longhand on plain, unruled cards. When she passed away, I inherited her recipe box stuffed full of cards and clippings from magazines. Grandma often made little notations in the borders: "Linda brought this April 23, 1967." "McNulty reunion Aug. 1–3." "Received with Terry's Christmas card 1984." "Johnny here en route to Winnipeg." I remembered eating Grandma's hermits, but I had not come across the recipe in that little box.

"Did you make her hermits very often?" I asked.

"No," said Anne, "I mostly make cake." She nodded toward the kitchen and I understood that I was to enjoy her *apfelkuchen* this evening. "Would you like me to send you the recipe?"

It was agreed that I would receive through the mail the recipes for Grandma Jo's hermits and Anne's *apfelkuchen*. The evening was off to an auspicious start. I returned to the table with this good news.

"We have an in," I said. "The lady overseeing the mustard contest knew my grandma."

"Of course she did," said John. Since moving to Saskatchewan, he had come to the conclusion that I could walk into any crowd and find a relative or, failing that, a relative by one degree of separation. In this observation, he is largely correct.

"Is she the judge?" he asked.

"No," I said. "It's a taste test. Everyone votes."

"So, how does that give you an in?"

"It's good karma."

"Mustard does not have karma."

I was about to protest when we were interrupted by the rumble of a microphone. The polka band had stepped down and an angular fellow in a red vest and bowtie was on the stage making an announcement about the upcoming Beer Barrel Rolling Contest. Following a general description of this athletic event, he called for contestants to sign up.

"Especially you young people in the room." He looked our way. Despite being no spring chickens ourselves, we were among the youngest in attendance that evening. (Though it would become evident with the dancing that we were *not* among the most spry!) I was quite happy to sit this one out as I would rather swallow my beer than play with it, but John informed me that he had already signed us up, "since we're not worried about bad hips and trick knees," he said.

A choir of women in dirndl skirts and trachten jackets took the stage, bursting into a spirited rendition of "I Love to Go A-wandering" to the accompaniment of a robust accordion. "Everyone join in," called the lead lady, but since they sang in German I could only hum along. My mind wandered with the music to alpine meadows, high grassy pastures beneath snowy peaks, cattle wearing clunky copper bells, herders in leather lederhosen and blousy shirts and maidens in white aprons tied over embroidered skirts. Sure, things have changed since *The Sound of Music*, but the romantic image of alpine costume was alive and well and subject to a good deal of improvisation in the hall that evening – lederhosen made from corduroy pants cut off at the knees, homemade dirndl skirts lined with embroidered ribbon, clip-on suspenders and shiny silver buttons sewed onto fitted vests.

A fellow at the next table stood and cried out the German toast *"Eins, zwei, drei, g'suffa!"* We raised our glasses and drank together. Suddenly, it was a party. The polka band was playing again, and couples took to the dance floor with the grace and compatibility that only years of stepping out together can bring. "It's just like the Jubilee Hall in Munroe, Wisconsin," declared John. While he may be unwilling to dance the polka, he is perfectly happy to sit and *suffa* to the music.

Talk turned to his university days at the University of Wisconsin–LaCrosse and the "kegger" parties back when a keg cost just five dollars. (It was, after all, Wisconsin where a proposal to tax beer was met with such public outrage that the politicians had to about-face or lose face.) I recalled the time I was in Munich during Oktoberfest, drinking a mug of beer so huge it had to be hoisted with two hands, in a tent so large you had to squint to see the far end, surrounded by a crush of people that might have outnumbered the everyday population of Humboldt, Saskatchewan. In the centre of the tent was a raised stage on which a swing band played popular songs from the forties and fifties. Caught up in the spirit of the music, an old German fellow across my table lifted his glass toward a group of American servicemen, declaring with good cheer, "When this song was popular, we were bombing the hell out of each other! Ha!" With that, both he and the servicemen took a good long *suffa* to each other's health.

Now the fellow in the red bow tie was back at the microphone calling on the contestants in the Beer Barrel Rolling Contest. Two L-shaped lines had been marked on the floor with black tape, and the first two contestants took their marks at the start line, each one poised over an empty silver keg. At the sound of the gun, they set off rolling their kegs along the tape, turning more or less adroitly at the "L" and dashing madly over the finish line. John handled the barrel like an old "kegger" pro. Murray deftly negotiated his keg first over the finish line. Heather bested her opponent with speed and grace. As for me, I lost grip of my keg at the kink in the road and recovered only by hoisting the barrel into my arms and walking it over the line. Win or lose, we were each awarded a souvenir beer mug, which was promptly christened in a toast to good friends.

The exertion rekindled our appetites, and we made our way through the swirling couples to the adjacent hall, where the local sausage makers were offering a taste of their wares. If I had to name one food that is quintessentially Saskatchewan – a food that traverses our diverse geographies and ethnic cuisines, a food with a long history and, I hope, an even longer future – it would be the humble sausage. In Saskatchewan, we do sausage very well. German *weisswurst*, Polish koubasa, breakfast sausage, farmer's sausage, beef jerky, beer sticks, venison pepperoni, bison wieners, even a juicy sausage made with cherries in the mix. As I nibbled my way from table to table, I couldn't help but think that each and every one of these lovely sausages would go well with a dab of Penny's mustard, and even better with Penny's *award-winning* mustard. It was time to vote.

There were six entries on the mustard table, each one removed from its original vessel and placed in identical glass bowls marked with a number from one to six. I gave each one a critical eye, moving first from right to left and then from left to right. I got in closer and gave each a sniff, then tipped each bowl this way and that into the light. After several minutes of intense scrutiny befitting a csi detective, I had to confess that I was stumped. I had no idea which one was Penny's mustard.

Each one was identical to the next. Smooth, not grainy, the colour of turmeric with little red flecks and thick like honey. No hearty brown mustard. No yellow hot dog condiment. Not a grainy mustard seed in sight. It was the Dijon Quintuplets of mustard, with an extra one thrown in for good measure. If I had not been rejected by Penny herself, I might have sworn she had shared her old family recipe with the entire town of Humboldt.

Obviously, I would have to investigate beyond the visual clues. Looks can be deceiving; the proof is in the pudding. One by one, I spread a dab of mustard on a cracker and gave it a slow, thoughtful analysis on the four corners of my mouth. I shut my eyes, summoning the tactile and taste memory of Penny's mustard, contrasting the imprint on my taste buds with the sensation on my tongue. Then I opened my eyes and raised my head in complete assurance that Penny's mustard was Number 5. I wrote the number on a ballot paper and dropped it in the box.

"Did you vote?" I asked John. He was sampling a breakfast sausage.

"Yes, I did."

"Did you vote for Penny's mustard?"

"Of course. Number 3."

"Three! I can't believe it! Penny's mustard is Number 5."

"Well, I voted for Number 3."

"Did you vote for Number 3 because you liked it best, or because you *thought* it was Penny's mustard?"

"Both," he said. "Are you so sure it was Number 5?"

When Heather and Murray returned from a spin on the dance floor, I pressed them to reveal their votes. Heather had voted for Number 1. Murray for Number 6. Imagine that! I suppose they could be forgiven – after all, they had not had the pleasure of tasting Penny's mustard before that evening. But what was John's excuse? How could he be so diametrically wrong? Why hadn't I escorted him to the mustard table to supervise his vote? I should have hovered like a two-bit dictator until he had cast his ballot for Number 5. Instead, we had cancelled each other out.

The polka band had finished its gig and a DJ with a case of music was setting up on the stage. He blew a fuse with the first song, plunging the hall into darkness. It seemed like a good time to gather up our coats and our beer mugs and, yes, my wounded pride, and slip out of the party for the long drive home. Since the mustard contest closed at midnight, I would not know the outcome until the morrow. I had not given up hope.

The following day, I placed a call to the organizer of the Humboldt Oktoberfest to learn the results of the Homemade Mustard Contest. The winner, she informed me, was Number 3.

"And whose mustard was that?" I asked.

"Well," she gave a little laugh, "it was mine."

"Congratulations," I said, trying not to imply by tone or inflection that she had won the mustard contest any way but fair and square.

"And could you tell me, please, what number was my entry?"

There was a short pause while she looked it up. "You were Number 5."

I knew it! What a relief. While I would have to concede that John had picked a winner, my own taste buds had been true. I saw no need to hold grudges.

"Would you mind," I pressed, "sharing your mustard recipe with me?"

"I don't think I could do that," she said.

"Why? Because it's a secret family recipe?"

"Oh, no," she chuckled, "because I didn't use a recipe. A little of this, a little of that. I just whipped it up."

It would be a long winter without Penny's mustard. Hamburger season turned to meatloaf season turned to turkey season, but I did not lose heart. Mustard karma was on my side. When John asked what I wanted for Christmas, I smiled sweetly and told him, "Nothing that money can buy, honey, nothing that money can buy."

# BRING OUT THE WURST

SOMETIMES WE BUY a kitchen gadget with every intention of using it, frequently, only to discover it years later, still in the original packaging, unused. I suspect this is the fate of many a pasta roller and ice cream maker (though I do use mine). No, the tool I bought and forgot was the sausage stuffing attachment for my Kitchen Aid.

My husband has a soft spot for sausage. He attributes this to his upbringing in a part of Wisconsin settled by Swiss and German farmers with their traditional *wurst* – *weisswurst*, *knockwurst*, *blutwurst*, bratwurst. Every summer, he hosts a Sausage Fest in our backyard to which his guests are asked not to BYOB (he supplies the beer) but to BYOSS: Bring Your Own Saskatchewan Sausage. This brings out the best of the *wurst*. Locally made ham sausage, koubasa, farmers' sausage, garlic coil, bison smokies, venison bratwurst and beer sticks; Spanish chorizo, Lebanese lamb kebabs, French *merguez* and Balkan *cévapčiči*. And John's Wisconsin favourite, brats boiled in beer and onions. Lined up on the barbeque, it's a mini United Nations of the sausage world.

Yet we never made sausage until we met Ralph. Ralph's dad was a German butcher, so he grew up with a sixth sense for meat. We carted the Kitchen Aid, with its meat grinder and sausage stuffer attachments, over to Ralph and Lisa's house and we made sausage: spicy Italian, koubasa (which he later smoked), breakfast and bratwurst with a mixture of pork and venison. It's been said that, if you like sausage, you should never watch them being made. I disagree. If you observe the process, it just makes you fussier about the quality of the ingredients that go inside. Only the best for our *wurst*.

## JOHN'S WISCONSIN BRATS

In Wisconsin, where beer is considerably less expensive, John boils the brats in straight beer. Since moving to Saskatchewan, he mixes it with water. Such are the compromises made for love.

| | |
|---|---|
| 2 | bottles of beer |
| 6 | bratwurst |
| 2 | big onions, sliced |
| 2 tbsp | grainy mustard |
| | Water to cover |
| 1 tbsp | butter (optional) |

Place the beer, bratwurst, onions and mustard in a pot. Add enough water to cover. Bring to a boil until the brats are cooked. Place the brats on a hot grill to brown on both sides. If you like (this step is good but optional) scoop the onions from the beer and sauté in butter. Serve the brats on good bakery hot dog buns topped with the onions. If, as at Sausage Fest, you need to cook more brats, feel free to reuse the beer broth.

# HOT GERMAN POTATO SALAD

John is a master at making traditional cold potato salad for a summer's day, but on a wintery evening it's nicer to eat hot potatoes.

| 4 | slices of bacon |
|---|---|
| 6 cups | potatoes, sliced ¼ inch thick |
| | Chives, chopped |

DRESSING

| ½ cup | onion, chopped |
|---|---|
| 2 tbsp | flour |
| 2 tbsp | sugar |
| ½ tsp | mustard powder |
| 1 tsp | celery seed |
| | Salt and pepper to taste |
| 1 cup | water |
| ½ cup | white wine vinegar |

Cook the bacon until crisp. Cool and crumble. To make the dressing, cook the onion in the bacon drippings. If the bacon was lean and there's not enough fat to cook the onions, add a bit of butter. Sprinkle with the flour, sugar, mustard powder, celery seed and a dash of salt and pepper. Give it a good stir to fully incorporate the flour. Add the water and vinegar; cook over low heat until thick and bubbly.

Meanwhile, cook the sliced potatoes in plenty of salted water. Drain. Place the potatoes in a serving bowl. Pour the dressing onto the hot potatoes, along with the crumbled bacon, and stir gently to coat the potatoes without breaking them to pieces. Garnish with chopped chives. Eat it while it's warm.

# ANNE'S APFELKUCHEN

Anne says she's had this *apfelkuchen* recipe for so long she can't remember where she got it. My apologies to the source, whoever you might be.

CAKE

| | |
|---|---|
| 1 cup | butter or margarine |
| ½ cup | sugar |
| 2 | eggs, room temperature |
| 1 tsp | vanilla |
| ¼ tsp | salt |
| 1 tsp | baking powder |
| 1 ¾ cup | flour |

TOPPING

| | |
|---|---|
| 5 | large tart apples, peeled and sliced |
| 1 cup | sugar |
| 1 tsp | cinnamon |
| ⅔ cup | cake batter |
| ⅔ cup | flour |

Cream the butter and sugar. Add the eggs one at a time and mix well. Mix in the vanilla, salt, baking powder and flour. Remove ⅔ cup of cake batter for the topping. Press the remaining batter into a greased 9 x 12 inch pan. (Or a smaller pan for a thicker cake.)

Cover the batter with sliced, peeled apples. Sprinkle the apples evenly with sugar and cinnamon. Mix the reserved batter with the flour until it resembles coarse crumbs. Spread over the apples. Bake at 350° F for 45 minutes, until the top is light brown. Anne suggests serving it with cream.

# 10
## FALL VERSUS FOWL

### A DICKENS OF A CHRISTMAS GOOSE

AROUND HERE, we say tomato not tom*aaa*to and potato not pot*aaa*to, but we can't seem to reach common consensus on what to call that institution of prairie gastronomy, the fall supper – or is it the fowl supper? By long-standing tradition, these popular community dinners fill the seasonal calendar between harvest time and Christmas Tea and Craft Sales, thus the fall designation. Also by long-standing tradition, the centrepiece of the meal is a bird – turkey or chicken – and thus the fowl designation. Whether fall or fowl, the meal is guaranteed to be good old-fashioned down-home cooking at its best. In other words, comfort food.

It was the fall of 1994 and my future husband had just moved to Saskatchewan. I was acquainting him with the highlights of prairie living, which naturally included that annual showcase of prairie hospitality, *the* social event of the season: a fall/fowl supper.

John is no stranger to community dinners, but – and this is their universal appeal – authentic community dinners vary from place to place depending on the local, cultural and seasonal milieu. He hails from southwest Wisconsin, where the flavours are decidedly more Scandinavian than here in Saskatchewan, where East European sauerkraut meets British roast beef. So, while he's an old hand at navigating the buffet table, his dinner plate was more familiar with lutefisk, lefse and Swedish meatballs than with perogies, cabbage rolls and raisin pie.

Choosing which fall/fowl supper to attend is like choosing between movies when all the blockbusters are out. Every one looks good. But choose one must. Given our busy orientation schedule, I narrowed the field by selecting a Saturday in October when we had no other plans for dinner. I narrowed it further by deciding on a small-town supper rather than a city affair. After all, my goal was to introduce him to the fabric of prairie culture, and that fabric is woven in the countryside. Mind you, not *too* far in the countryside, since we would be driving home after dark under the influence of tryptophan and pie.

The modern conventions of websites, blogs and online directories have barely touched the traditional world of the fall/fowl supper. The best means of advertising is old-fashioned word of mouth, particularly word from the pulpit, since fall/fowl suppers are often hosted by the local church. But for those wishing to spread the good word further afield – and for those of us seeking it – you can do no better than to turn to the listing of "Fun and Fellowship" in the Religion Section of the Saturday newspaper. There, my attention was drawn to the St. Aloysius parish fall supper in the town of Allan, about an hour's drive away. The time and the location fit the bill. I marked it on the calendar and circled the date.

The day of the St. Aloysius fall supper was frosty and grey. Big snowflakes wafted through the air like feathers, giving the quiet countryside a lonely charm. Along the drive, I warmed up our taste buds by recounting all the wonderful foods one might encounter at a fall/fowl supper. Turkey, but maybe chicken or roast beef or, in a French-speaking parish, tourtière. Mashed potatoes and gravy or, in a Ukrainian community, perogies stuffed with potatoes or cabbage rolls stuffed with rice, or all three. On the side, there might be bread stuffing, creamed corn, pickled beets, bread-and-butter pickles and – if perogies were being served – silky onions sautéed in butter, with a dollop of sour cream.

For salads, one could expect coleslaw and any one or more of the following: pasta salad, bean salad, potato salad, jelly salad or lettuce greens. Buns, preferably homemade, and butter. And for dessert, various pies – apple, saskatoon, raisin, lemon meringue, pumpkin or cherry – and, if you were lucky, a scoop of too-soft ice cream on top. I could already smell the peppery gravy and the fresh-perked coffee, and I'm quite sure I heard a rumble in John's tummy...or was that mine?

We arrived in Allan at five o'clock, early enough, I hoped, to beat the lineup at the buffet table; but if not, I was prepared to suffer the wait with patience and good humour, striking up a conversation with the next person on a pertinent topic such as the weather or the lovely selection of salads. But as we pulled into the parking lot of the communiplex at dusk, I couldn't help but notice it was strangely deserted. Where I had expected to see rows and rows of cars in a fog of exhaust, children pouring out of back seats, parents carrying toddlers in snow-suits and old people clutching each other's arms for the slippery walk through the beam of headlights, there were just a couple of frosty cars and a single solitary light over the front door.

"Perhaps the hall is at the back of the building," I said. I drove a loop around the communiplex, but there were fewer cars out back than there were out front. "Perhaps supper was moved to the church hall."

"You'd think they'd put up a sign," said John.

"Probably everyone in town already knows," I said. "Word of mouth."

We drove down Main Street, which was just as deserted as the parking lot of the communiplex. The whole town had gone indoors. Curtains were drawn and white puffs curled up from the chimneys. Over the rooftops, I spied a white church steeple and drove around to face it, parked and got out of the car. St. Aloysius was still and quiet but, just to be sure, I walked up the front steps and tried the door. Locked up tight. I got back into the car, panic replacing hunger in the pit of my stomach.

"Maybe you got the time wrong," said John. "Maybe it starts at six."

We drove back to the communiplex. There were several more cars in the parking lot, and I dared to think that John was right. We were simply early. At that very moment, turkeys were warming in ovens all over town while potatoes were being mashed and gravy was bubbling away on the stove. Soon the church ladies would begin arriving with their salads and pies. Another car pulled up and parked, but instead of a hustling woman with a casserole cradled in her arms, it was an older gent in a tweed cap with a broom and a pair of curling shoes slung over his shoulder. We followed him inside.

The room was as bright and familiar as any small town curing rink. Plywood floors, white walls, fluorescent lights, a big wooden bench facing the picture windows that overlook the ice. On the wall, a case full of trophies topped with gleaming little men and women crouched in the curler's pose, foot in the hack and low to the ice. On the opposite wall, a counter opened onto the kitchen, and an opening on the far side of the kitchen looked onto the foyer of the hockey rink. Burgers were sizzling on the grill. The gentleman with the curling broom said "G'd evening" to a couple of senior ladies who were chatting on the bench, then disappeared through a side door that led to the ice.

"Excuse me," I interrupted the two ladies, who were deep in conversation about somebody's turn of bad health, "is this the venue of the fowl supper?"

"You mean the St. Aloysius Fall Supper?" asked the silver-haired woman, raising a perfectly manicured eyebrow.

"Yes," I said. "The annual St. Aloysius Fall Supper."

"Yes," she said, pointing. "It's through that door."

"Yes," said the other one. "Through that door. Tomorrow."

"Tomorrow?"

"Always on a Sunday."

"Better not be tonight, because my turkey is as cold as a curling rock!"

They laughed, but the joke was on me. Oh, yes, I could just hear them telling this one to their friends at coffee row on Monday morning. Did you hear about the city slickers who came for the fall supper on the wrong night? What a turkey! Her goose was cooked! And a fowl time was had by all! I felt as small as the silver lass atop a curling trophy. I confessed to John what had become so painfully obvious: I had the right time and the right venue but the wrong night.

"Well, we're here," he said, "and I'm hungry. Let's eat."

I left John leaning against the benches and sidled up to the kitchen counter. A sullen teenager took my order: cheeseburgers and fries, plus a couple of coffees. She was wearing enough eye makeup for a nightclub (had she been old enough to get in the door) and big bangle earrings. As she poured the coffee, a fellow in an apron slapped our burgers onto the grill. I knew the scenario in an instant. The fellow in the apron was no doubt her father who had volunteered her for the family's turn at the community rink concession stand. Perhaps her boyfriend was playing hockey and she'd rather be fluttering her eyelashes at the game. Or maybe the car keys hung in the balance. I wanted to say, "Cheer up honey, I just drove an hour for these cheeseburgers. Let's make the best of it." And while it wasn't exactly the healthy home-cooked community dinner I had been anticipating, it was a meal that evoked my childhood just the same.

Growing up, I spent many an hour at the curling rink. Curling was part of the high school phys. ed. curriculum, and I played in the annual funspiel. My dad curled a lot, and when my three younger siblings were old enough, they formed a foursome and curled together. From an early age, I knew the ins and outs of in-turns and out-turns, the meaning of "draw weight" and what to do when ordered to "Hurraaayyy Haaaaaard!" That is not to say I *liked* curling. It seemed a bit odd to come in from the ice and cold to play in the ice and cold. Wouldn't it make more sense to curl in the summer when you actually *needed* cooling down?

John, on the other hand, had absolutely no clue about curling (despite the fact that Wisconsin is the US hotbed of curling – if that's not a contradiction in terms). Even so, when I got back to the bench with our burgers, he was deep in conversation with the two ladies, who were explaining the game so far.

"The red team stole the first end."

"Now it's the lead shot. He's going to give it a left curl and place a guard just inside the hog line."

The skip stood with his back to us, his curling broom tapping the spot on the ice where he hoped the rock would stop. At the far end, the fellow in the tweed cap gave the rock a gentle swing and sent it idling towards us.

"The ice is very slow tonight."

"Looks like his new knee is holding out..."

The two sweepers bent into the task, dashing their brooms back and forth across the ice in front of the rock, bringing it to rest just over the hog line. The skip gave a "good shot" wave to the guy at the far end.

"What's so good about that?" asked John. "It's nowhere near the bull's eye."

"It's a guard," said the silver-haired lady. "The next shot will come in behind and kiss the house."

The other team did just that, placing a rock on the edge of the red circle. The guy in the tweed cap launched his second rock like a rocket. The sweepers held off, sliding along beside it until they got the nod from the skip. "Hurraaayyy Haaaaaard!" They swept the ice frantically until the rock came to a crashing halt against that of their opponent, knocking it out of the house.

"Why do they sweep?" John asked his new-found guide to curling. "If it's going that fast, what's the point?"

I wondered if, when the game was invented in Scotland all those years ago, the founding fathers had debated whether to call it curling or sweeping, because the two are inextricably connected to the game. I suppose "sweeping" sounds too much like housework.

"They sweep to keep up the speed," she explained, "so the rock doesn't curl too much."

John absorbed this information. "So, they sweep *in front* of the rock so it goes *faster*?"

She deftly explained this seeming incongruity – that the sweeping action warms the pebbles, making them smoother and slipperier, and thus the rock travels faster and straighter.

"Pebbles?" asked John.

She looked at him. "Where are you from, anyway?"

John gave them his story, how he grew up in Darlington in Lafayette County, Wisconsin, and how he followed his heart to Saskatchewan. How he was raised on football and baseball, but not this strange sport of curling, which looked like a cross between winter lawn bowling and frozen shuffleboard. Once, he spent a whole day watching cricket in a town in England with a fellow who explained every move, yet the next day he couldn't for the life of him remember the rules. Sports are like that. More cultural than logical. I suggested we cap our coffees and head back to the city.

"Can we stay for this round?" he asked.

"The *end*," I corrected him.

"No, we don't have to stay to the end. Just a few more shots. I think I'm getting the hang of it."

IN THE DEBATE between the fall supper and fowl supper, we must look beyond the conveniences of modern gastronomy to a time when a bird was just a bird. To a time before pre-stuffed, pop-up, self-basting, flash-frozen, water-injected and best-before dates. Back when the fowl lived a happy life scratching in the earth and eating kitchen scraps, and met its fate at the hands of the one who would later sit down to eat it. In other words, a bird whose life cycle – from baby chick to grandma's china – unfolded on the family farm.

It is no wonder those first fowl suppers landed in the fall. The flock was dispatched in fall just as Mother Nature provided a freezer as big as all outdoors. It was only natural to pop one of those freshly plucked birds into the oven and to serve it up with the rest of fall's bounty. And just as natural still, to get together with your neighbours to share the feast and celebrate another harvest well done.

In keeping with this pioneer spirit, I decided to throw a fowl supper the old-fashioned way. I would pluck vegetables from my own garden. Bake pies with fruit I picked myself. Make bread with fresh-milled flour and churn the butter from real farm cream. At the centre of the meal would be a bird I had dispatched myself. From start to finish, dinner would be a testament to the goodness and gratification of food procured by my own hands.

This project appealed to me on a number of levels. At its very base, it was an exercise in self-sufficiency; if I had to, I could fend for myself. It was also an exercise in reality; it's too easy to forget in these days of styrofoam trays and plastic wrap that, for the most part, the meat we eat comes from an animal that lived, and died, for the sole purpose of gracing our dinner plates. However, while I had plucked many a chicken in my youth, I had never dispatched one by my own hand. (Dad and his axe took care of that.) This seemed a gap in my participation in the food chain. If I was going to be a well-informed and conscientious food consumer, I should be engaged in the process from start to stomach. At least once.

I needed a bird. My dad no longer kept chickens on the family farm, and I hadn't attempted to raise a few surreptitious birds in my backyard in the city. In Europe and Asia, it is not uncommon to see live chickens for sale in the farmers' markets, but I had not found them even wrapped and frozen at a farmers' market close to home. I knew a few farmers who raised poultry, but would they let me loose with an axe anywhere near their chicken coop? I was ruminating on this dilemma when the answer arrived in my inbox. It was an invitation to take part in a waterfowl hunt.

Now, who says the fowl had to be farmed? A wild fowl was plenty fowl enough for me. A duck or a coot or a goose would do the trick for Thanksgiving dinner. Of course, I wouldn't be able to shoot the bird myself, since I lacked the credentials necessary to get a hunting licence, but I could take part in the hunt, "beat the bush" as they say in hunting lingo, and get my feet wet, literally. Later, I would take the hunter safety course and, with any luck, qualify for a hunting licence before the season was through. Then I would set my sights on a new goal: to bag a goose for an old-fashioned, heartwarming, Dickensian Christmas dinner.

On hunting day, the weather was clearly on the side of the ducks: chilly and wet. There was no sign of the moon or stars as I drove out of the city well before dawn with the wipers flapping and the headlights on high. I had picked up another hunter, a university student named Katherine, who was dressed for the occasion in a lovely camouflage ensemble with matching toque, accessorized with a new shotgun in a padded case. I, on the other hand, was wearing a mishmash of outdoor gear, including my husband's raincoat and hip waders which, despite the layers of sweaters and longjohns underneath, were so roomy I was swimming in them, which was appropriate given the weather.

Despite all that, my spirits were not the least bit damp. This was an adventure of the best sort – one that resulted, at the end of the day, in something good to eat. Perhaps our hunting party would bag a bird or two, but if not, I would suffer no culinary disappointment because I had been invited to attend a waterfowl luncheon at the Saskatoon Gun Club after the hunt. The menu, I was told, included coot *cassoulet*, crane wraps and barbecued duck breast wrapped in bacon. No matter how wet and cold I might get on the outside, I was buoyed by the assurance that afterwards there would be something warm and yummy to comfort my inside.

Our destination that morning was the farm of Sue and Vance, two avid hunters who live an hour's drive from the city on the highway to Biggar. This is a neat coincidence since, as every big game hunter knows, Biggar is the home of the legendary Hanson Buck, the largest whitetail deer in the Boone and Crockett record books. The antlers of the Hanson Buck are so large they shattered the old record set in 1914 by the Jordan Buck of Wisconsin. If you're not a hunter, you could be forgiven for not grasping the enormity of this achievement. The Hanson Buck is an A-list celebrity, housed in an undisclosed vault, portraitized in limited-edition wildlife prints and immortalized in plastic with the Hunter Dan action doll. Among game hunters, the Hanson Buck is more famous than Bambi.

Not being a hunter, I was quite oblivious to the Hanson Buck phenomenon until John called me from Wisconsin, where, among his hunting buddies, the Hanson Buck was all the buzz. Thanks to his tip, and to my job at CBC Television, I found myself in Biggar for the official measurement for the Boone and Crockett record books. By the end of the day, the town of Biggar had once again lived up to its slogan – "New York Is Big, But This Is Biggar" – by earning a vaulted place in the annals of hunting history.

This morning, however, we would not be venturing as far as Biggar. Our destination was closer to the town of Perdue. (Where the slogan is *not* "If You're Here, You're Lost." Word has it, Perdue was not named for the French word for lost, but after a popular judge.) Since I had been to Sue and Vance's farm once before, I had a rough idea of where I was going. But that had been a bright sunny day, and now it was black and raining. I couldn't recognize any of the landmarks as the wipers swished back and forth and the headlights blazed a tunnel through the dark night. I knew if we arrived at Perdue we were, if not entirely lost, definitely too far down the road.

One u-turn and a couple of false leads later, we pulled into their farm at the first grey light of dawn. We were greeted by their bird dog, Belle, a large munsterlander who seemed to be well aware we were joining her for a hunt. The rain had tapered off to a soaking mist as the four of us – Sue, Katherine, Belle and I – set off in good spirits across the pasture, stopping to nuzzle a couple of affectionate horses, ducking through a barbed wire fence (carefully handing the guns over first, all rules of hunting safety strictly observed) and down to a little duck pond at the far side of the farm. Sue and Katherine each carried a shotgun, while I, having not yet earned my firearms certificate, was relegated to carrying a thermos of hot coffee.

We settled into a bed of tall grass in the shelter of a willow bush and waited for the ducks. The wind had picked up, making little riffles on the water. Katherine crouched at the ready with the shotgun at her side. Sue kept a hand on Belle's collar, Belle twitching every muscle in the conflict between obedience and the chase. And I sat stoically in the middle, wiping my wet face with the back of a damp glove and daydreaming of my fowl supper. Would it be a casserole of duck and wild rice? Honey duck with roast vegetables? Stuffed with mushrooms and apples? Or a sauce of cherries and mint? I could smell the mint already, but it was not my imagination. We had settled our butts (shotgun and otherwise) into a patch of wild mint, the odour of which permeated the air around us each time we shifted position as the minutes ticked by.

It was no small irony that, while we personified the saying "like water off a duck's back," there was not a duck in sight, evidence, no doubt, that even the ducks had the good sense to stay out of the rain. Had it been a sunny day, we would have spied great flocks of ducks and geese gathering for the long flight south. We might have even heard the echo of a shot or two rippling across the landscape. But today, the fall migration was grounded by the weather.

Belle, who had been waiting patiently for some action, gave her master a longing look with those big doe eyes, and Sue gave in. The dog trotted off to explore the pond with the calm composure of a crime scene investigator. A little sniff, an alert eye, a false lead, a promising clue. She doubled back, and then, spotting something of interest at the far side of the pond, disappeared behind a thicket of cattails and tall, dry grass. A moment later, out of the reeds came a silent flotilla of ducks swimming into open water. Katherine raised the shotgun to her shoulder. It was a perfect shot. I held my breath and waited for the crack of the gun.

Finally, I whispered, "Why don't you shoot?"

Katherine whispered back, "Can't shoot a sitting duck."

"Why not?" I asked. "Isn't that the whole point of sitting ducks? You can't miss."

"It's not sporting," she said. "Can't shoot until they fly."

Sporting? This wasn't a sport, it was dinner. I offered to scare the ducks into flight, but that wasn't sporting either. Meanwhile, Belle was doing her best to do what I could not. She ran to the opposite bank to wait for the ducks, but well before landing they turned adroitly and swam the other way, leaving Belle to pace the shoreline out of reach. Katherine lowered the shotgun. If I hadn't known better, I'd say the ducks were well aware of the consternation they were causing and were having a little laugh about it. All in fun, I guess, and if the ducks could be good sports about it then I suppose I could be, too. I poured a cup of coffee and passed it around. When an hour had passed, we lifted ourselves out of the mint, stretched our cold, stiff legs and walked back to the house.

Lucky for us, no one told Belle that sitting ducks were out of bounds. She disappeared into the rushes of another pond and a few moments later, trotted up with a young mallard in her maw, presenting it to Sue like a proud child. The duck was alive and well. It looked at each of us without a peep.

"He's too young to fly," said Sue, gently cradling the duck in her arm. "Born too late to migrate south. He'll freeze to death."

"Or be eaten by a coyote," said Katherine.

"Not a nice way to go," said Sue with compassion. She took the duck by its head, gave it a good hard neck-breaking shake and carried it back to the house upside down by its skinny legs. With the same matter-of-fact efficiency, she spread a black garbage bag on the kitchen floor, plucked the feathers over the duck's breast, rolled off the tender white skin with her fingers and cut the breasts off the bone with a sharp hunting knife. She sprinkled them with Cajun spice and plunked them on the barbecue next to her famous duck breasts wrapped in bacon, which were destined for the Gun Club luncheon. A prehistoric hunter could not have accomplished the job with more efficiency and care, and I imagine we devoured those succulent little breasts with the same appreciation as the hunter's family – minus perhaps the Cajun spice.

This succulent appetizer, along with plenty of fresh air, had worked on my appetite. No matter that we had done nothing but sit for most of the morning; I can attest that sitting in the damp cold is exhausting work. By the time we arrived at the waterfowl luncheon, my tummy was rumbling. A steaming bowl of stew (say, a *cassoulet* of beans, pork and wild coot) would hit the spot.

A few years earlier, I ate an authentic *cassoulet* (that is, made with goose) in a little French village in the Black Hills, which counts among my top ten restaurant meals. I read in a French tourist brochure that the name "cassoulet" comes from the pot in which it is cooked, but no doubt some busy French cooks have made a passable *cassoulet* in that modern convenience known as a crockpot.

At the Gun Club, the coot *cassoulet* filled a crockpot. Next to it on the buffet table was a plate of tortilla wraps filled with grilled vegetables and nuggets of sandhill crane, and next to that, Sue's barbecue duck breasts wrapped in bacon. The atmosphere in the Gun Club sparkled with a kind of exhausted energy as dozens of hunters, a good many of them under the age of sixteen, filled their plates and sat down at wooden tables to eat their lunch. I sat down next to the picture window fogged over with heat and humidity, our damp clothes steaming and smelling of wet wool. A young lad beside me was picking at his plate like he would have preferred chicken nuggets or pizza instead.

"Which one do you like the best?" I asked with the intent of generating some enthusiasm.

He didn't look up from his plate. "I'm not sure what's what."

I pointed out each dish and gave it a short description.

"Coot *cassoulet*. Think of it as pork and beans. You like pork and beans?"

He nodded.

"Wraps with vegetables and sandhill crane. Looks like chicken, doesn't it?"

"Uh-huh."

"Well, it tastes like chicken. Nothing strange in that. And this is duck breast wrapped in bacon. Everything tastes better with bacon, right?"

He took a bite of the wrap and chewed on it awhile.

"Just think," I said, "if there was ever a disaster and Saskatoon was cut off from the world and food supplies couldn't get in, you'd be able to go out and hunt something good like this to eat."

He looked at me like I was nuts. Obviously, he was not learning to hunt so he could feed his family.

"I like fishing better," he said, swallowing hard.

MY FOWL SUPPER proceeded as planned except for one big exception – the fowl was a turkey purchased from Pine View Farms. No, I had not been the one to wring its neck, but I knew the farmers and I had been to their farm, and perhaps that is as close to the food chain as most city folks can hope to get. But it was not too late to get a Christmas goose.

I enrolled in a hunter education course which could be completed online at one's leisure, but unfortunately leisure was in short supply that fall. I had to dig the potatoes, hang the herbs and bring in the green tomatoes. Cream the corn, make raspberry syrup and apple-rosemary jelly. Turn the compost and rake the leaves. Hunting season came and went and I began to have second thoughts. Perhaps in the great continuum of life, I was ordained to be a farmer, not a hunter. To wield a hoe, not a gun.

Just as I pondered this dichotomy, another email from Sue arrived in my inbox. Good news! They had bagged a goose, which they had cleaned and breasted for me. I baked those goose breasts rolled around a stuffing of apples, potatoes and caraway seed and served them with creamed Brussels sprouts and puffy little mushroom *gougères*. It was not exactly the golden bird on the Cratchits' Christmas table, but a blessing all the same. In the debate between fall versus fowl, it seems my talents lean toward the fall harvest, not the fowl hunt. Perhaps I would do best to stick to my strengths and, rather than take up the hunt, cultivate good friends who do.

## THE DESIGNATED DRIVER

ON A FRIGID NEW YEAR'S DAY, my friend Vance asked if I would like a pheasant. Despite the lack of mercury, we were at his farm for an outdoor shinny tournament and wiener roast. He and Sue had recently gone hunting near Grasslands National Park where the pheasant were plentiful.

"It's not cleaned," he said.

"That's okay," I said. "John'll clean it."

---

FALL VERSUS FOWL

He put the pheasant in the back of my car. A few days later we met some friends for a drink and I told them about the pheasant in the back of my car. There's no point putting it in the freezer, I said, because it's much colder outside!

But when we returned to the car, the bird was gone. (When it's that cold, I don't lock the doors for fear of being frozen out.) Had someone stolen my pheasant? Impossible, I thought. Even a desperate thief wouldn't take a frozen bird complete with feathers and a head. Sure enough, I was right. We found the pheasant in the driver's seat, buckled in of course.

## CHICKEN CACCIATORE

*Cacciatore* (pronounced catch-a-tory) is Italian for hunter. Originally, I suppose it would have been made with a pheasant or hare, along with mushrooms and herbs picked during the hunt.

| | |
|---|---|
| 2 tbsp | canola oil |
| 1 | chicken, cut into pieces |
| | Salt and pepper |
| 1 | medium onion, chopped |
| 1 | green pepper, sliced |
| 2 | garlic cloves, chopped |
| ½ cup | dry red wine |
| | Handful of chopped herbs (such as rosemary, sage, thyme, oregano, parsley) |
| 10 | ripe tomatoes, chopped |

| 1 cup | mushrooms, chopped |
| | Hot cooked pasta of your choice |

In a heavy pot, heat the oil on medium high. Pat the chicken dry with paper towel, sprinkle with salt and pepper and brown on all sides. Using tongs, remove chicken and set aside.

Add onion, green pepper and garlic to the pot. Sauté until soft, stirring frequently. Pour in the wine. Simmer until the wine evaporates, scraping up any brown bits on the bottom of the pan.

Return the chicken to the pot along with the herbs, tomatoes and mushrooms. Add enough water to almost cover the chicken. Bring to a boil, then cover the pot, reduce the heat and simmer for two hours. Remove the lid and continue simmering until the sauce is thickened and rich in colour. Taste and add more spice or herbs as needed. To serve, it is customary to spoon the sauce onto pasta and place a piece of chicken on the side.

# RICOTTA PIE

While I love fall/fowl suppers, my favourite social gathering is the potluck supper – also a fine prairie tradition. For my contribution, I often take this savoury pie.

| | |
|---|---|
| 3 tbsp | fresh bread crumbs |
| | Butter for greasing the pan |
| 4 | eggs, room temperature |
| ¼ cup | flour |
| 1 tsp | dried herbs such as basil and oregano |
| | Salt and pepper |
| 2 cups | ricotta cheese |
| 3 | slices of crispy-cooked bacon, crumbled, or equivalent amount of ham |

Heat the oven to 400°F. Grease the inside of a pie plate with butter and sprinkle on the breadcrumbs to coat the bottom and sides.

Separate the eggs. Beat the yolks lightly, then mix in the flour, salt, pepper and herbs. Stir in the ricotta cheese and the bacon.

Beat the egg whites until fluffy but not too stiff and fold into the cheese mixture. Mix it gently to avoid deflating the whites. Spread the mixture into the pie plate and smooth the top. Bake for 20–25 minutes, until a brown crust has formed and a knife inserted in the centre comes out clean. Serve with chutney or caramelized onions.

# CARAMELIZED ONIONS

| 4–5 | large onions |
| ¼ cup | butter |
| ¼ cup | canola oil |
| 1 tbsp | balsamic vinegar |
| 1 tsp | salt |

Heat the butter and oil on medium low heat. While the butter is melting, cut the onions in half, then cut each half into thin slices. Stir the onion slices into the butter and oil so they are well coated. Sauté, covered, for about 30 minutes, until the onions are soft. Stir in the balsamic vinegar and salt. Turn the heat to low and cook, covered, for an hour or more. The onions should never dry out; add more oil if necessary. The onions are done when they are soft, creamy and brown.

# 11

## VIM AND VIGOUR

### THE TRUE NORTH STRONG AND FREE

- - - - - - - - - - - - - - - - - - - - - - - - - - - - - - - - - -

WHEN I WAS NINE, my grandparents sent me a post-card from the Canary Islands. On the backside, Grandpa wrote about a recent dinner, a Moroccan *diffa* of roast lamb, vegetables and "something like rice," which he and Grandma had eaten without the benefit of a knife and fork. "Just tear it to pieces," Grandpa wrote. He described how they rolled the food into bite-sized balls and popped them into their mouths.

This was quite intriguing to a farm kid from Saskatchewan. I could scarcely imagine my proper

---

grandparents sitting on pillows in a billowing tent eating from a communal bowl, but with their fingers? My parents were sticklers for table manners, and fingers were not considered eating utensils except perhaps for raw carrots and fried chicken. That my grandparents might so readily dispense with decorum in a foreign land opened my young imagination to the big wide world. They do things differently out there.

But it was not for the *diffa* that I pulled out that postcard over and over again in the dim light of my bedside lamp. It was the picture on the front of the card – four maidens in folk costume posing in a garden of pink bougainvillea and swaying palm trees, a snippet of blue sky peeping through the lush vegetation. A photo taken, according to the description, on Grand Canary Island. To a winterized prairie girl, it looked nothing short of paradise.

At nine, I knew all about palm trees. That past Christmas, Mom and Dad had piled their four children into the station wagon and driven through the snowdrifts to California to visit Uncle Guy and Aunt Daisy. We stayed in a motor motel with an outdoor pool where we swam by street light and ran barefoot on the grass. We waded in the ocean and ate oranges off the tree. We wore summer clothes and sneakers, and when the weather turned inclement, we donned rain coats and umbrellas, not parkas and mitts. Within a few days, I had a tan; within a week, I was ready to pack my Barbie and move.

There were palm trees everywhere. Tall leggy palms along the boulevards, squat fan-shaped palms in the parking lots of shopping malls and (as it was Christmas time) shaggy palms strung with coloured lights in the front yards of churches and ordinary homes. For me, those palm trees were the emblem of a land that winter forgot. Back in Saskatchewan, when the snow was blowing and the wind howling and the air so cold it prickled the skin, I knew that somewhere out there – far, far away – the maidens wore sandals even in December and a kid could enjoy winter without the benefit of a toque and a sled.

Don't get me wrong; winter was terrific on the farm. We built snow forts and made snow angels, went skating and rode our toboggans behind the snowmobile at dizzying speeds. I liked the way the trees around the farm sparkled white with hoarfrost against a cold mauve horizon, and how sundogs lit the sky at noon. I liked that cozy feeling of coming inside, peeling off the layers one by one and pressing my cold stockinged feet into the ribs of a warm radiator, feeling the blood tingle as the life returned to my cheeks and fingertips. If luck was on our side, we would be snowed in and miss school for more than one day in a row. There is no denying that the world is beautiful to a kid in winter.

No, it's not that I dislike winter, but by the end of February I have just about had enough of it. I know I shouldn't complain. There are many benefits to living in a northern climate. Nordic people are happier and live longer than folks in the tropics. In the north, there are fewer exotic diseases and venomous snakes. Southern crocodiles kill more people than northern bears. Excessive heat takes more lives than excessive cold. Tropical hurricanes are deadlier than temperate tornadoes and lightning combined. According to the surveys, Canada consistently ranks as one of the top ten happiest and healthiest countries in the world, right up there with Iceland and Sweden, and not a palm tree in sight.

Yes, we are a tough breed north of the 49th, and I am grateful to be blessed with a vigorous constitution and an optimistic frame of mind, but when it comes to winter, I freely admit, I am a bona fide wimp. As the sun goes down and the temperature with it, I want nothing more than to curl up in a quilt beside the fire and watch a movie on TV. As February rolls into March and winter shows no sign of melting away, that's where you'll find me, dreaming of palm trees and living the life of the common couch potato.

THIS IS NOT to malign the potato. A more vigorous and hard-working vegetable cannot be found. An acre of potatoes is four times more productive, in terms of calories, than an acre of wheat, and more nutritious, too. The potato is chock full of iron, potassium, calcium and vitamin C. Served with a bit of dairy, say, mashed with butter or baked with a dollop of sour cream, a potato is more nutritious than a slice of whole-wheat bread. When Europeans finally, reluctantly began eating potatoes in the 1700s, they found their populations grew healthier and lived longer than when they consumed a traditional diet based on grain. No one ate more potatoes than the Irish, and their population soared from two million in 1700 to 8.5 million by 1845, the year of the Great Potato Famine.

I gleaned these potato facts from a fascinating history of the spud by British writer John Reader, *Propitious Esculent: The Potato in World History*, which traces the path of the humble tuber from its home turf high up in the Andes Mountains of South America, across the ocean in the holds of Spanish galleons, overland through Europe and beyond – even to Mars, if NASA has its way.

Around the year 1770, the potato won a French competition to identify the best "food substances capable of reducing the calamities of famine." Marie Antoinette was apparently quite fond of them, and no doubt she would have lived to a healthy old age if she hadn't lost her head. Perhaps if she had said, "Let them eat spuds," things might have turned out differently.

Lest the Irish potato famine besmirch the potato's good name, Mr. Reader makes it perfectly clear that the potato did not cause the famine; it was the victim of a fungal invasion that ravaged the crop during a particularly wet couple of years. Not only did it wipe out the potatoes in the field, it rotted the potatoes in storage so there were none to plant when the conditions improved. Potatoes were also the victim of monoculture – growing one crop so intensively on so much land made it vulnerable to an enemy with no known prevention. Since the Irish ate almost nothing but potatoes, it hit them particularly hard. This is one of the ironic twists of history – if it hadn't been for the blessing of the potato, there would not have been so many Irish to suffer its loss.

From the moment the potato arrived in Europe in the mid-1500s, it suffered a severe crisis of character. Doctors warned it caused leprosy and gout (because it *looked* like leprosy and gout). Clerics said it was ungodly (because it wasn't mentioned in the Bible) and aroused the sins of laziness and lust. The Russians called it the devil's apple, and in 1748, the Parliament of France passed a law against eating a potato of any kind. The *Encyclopædia Britannica* of 1768 described the potato as a "demoralizing esculent."

As for the French, who have long considered themselves the arbiters of gastronomic good taste, there was even less enthusiasm for the potato. The famous French gourmand Jean-Anthelme Brillat-Savarin soundly panned the spud: "I appreciate the potato only as a protection against famine; except for that, I know of nothing more eminently tasteless." In other words, it may be good for you, but that doesn't make it *good*. As a food, the potato was considered fit for no one but paupers and pigs. If you had to eat potatoes it meant you were hopelessly down and out.

Perhaps it didn't help that the potato is poisonous. The green parts – the leaves, the stems and even the tuber, if it has turned green – contain a bitter toxin designed by nature for the very purpose of preventing consumption. This is a holdover from its wild days when the bitter taste kept predators away. It is hard to imagine how the human predator (that is, the first farmers to grow and eat potatoes some eight thousand years ago) managed to breed a tuber that wasn't bitter and poisonous since the only measure was a taste test. Perhaps they drew straws and took their chances for the good of the whole.

I like to think the potato was complicit in this arrangement, that it freely gave up its defences in exchange for world domination. In less than five hundred years, the potato has spread its roots to the four corners of the globe. Nowadays, China is the largest producer of potatoes, and the people of Rwanda eat more potatoes per capita than in its homeland of Peru. In terms of sheer volume, Ireland ranks below India and Iran. The potato is the most popular vegetable in North America, thanks to a little technique we picked up from the French.

Sure enough, somewhere between the high Andes and global conquest, Europeans lost their distaste for the potato. A short time after it triumphed as the most likely of "food substances capable of reducing the calamities of famine," the medical academy in Paris gave it a good bill of health. The rich and famous of European aristocracy began serving it at hoity-toity dinners – the guest list at one celebrated feast included King Louis xvi, his wife, Marie Antoinette and the American envoy Benjamin Franklin – at which it was trendy to feature potatoes in every course of the meal.

The humble potato simply needed dressing up. It needed the regalia of cream and caviar, cosseted with eggs and cheese, accessorized with onions and bacon, perfumed with nutmeg and cumin, pampered in hot ovens and deep fryers. Like the fine ladies of Versailles applying their wigs and white powder, the potato profited greatly from a bit of tarting up. Thus today we have such culinary treasures as potato perogies, shepherd's pie, Spanish omelette, potato salad, tartiflette, curry aloo, latkes, rösti, raclette, gnocchi and vichyssoise. Who can imagine vegetable samosas without potatoes? Or fast food without french fries? What is ham without scalloped potatoes or turkey gravy without mashed? Who hasn't warmed up to a baked potato or curled up on the couch with a bag of ripple chips?

So, here we are back on the couch.

On the Internet, I found an interesting explanation for the term "couch potato": A group of fellows from California who watched a lot of television (i.e., the boob tube) called themselves "tubers" which, of course, is the botanical name given to the swollen edible root of potatoes and yams. Following this logic, "tubers" who planted themselves on the couch to watch television became "couch potatoes." This is a clever play on words, if a shameful slander of a vegetable that deserves our utmost respect. But it raises an important question: If I lounge like a couch potato because it's -30 outside, what's their excuse in California? And if palm trees aren't the cure for the couch, have I been pining for a false flora all these many years? Perhaps I would do better to emulate the potato and learn to accept my naturally ordained place in life.

The truth is, the potato is right at home in Saskatchewan. It thrives in the hot, dry summers and, given a cool place to hang out, will patiently sit tight through the winter months. Come spring, it's raring to go. Nary a sniffle or complaint. If we could survey the adult potato population of Saskatchewan, we would no doubt find that they, too, are happier and healthier than their counterparts to the south. Indeed, scientific evidence is backing this up. New research shows that potatoes grown at a northern latitude have a certain vigour, a virtuosity, a *joie de vivre* not found in southern spuds.

This is called northern vigour. When northern potatoes are planted at southern latitudes, they grow more vigorously and produce more spuds than tubers originating in the south. Put another way, potatoes grown in Saskatchewan and planted in Idaho, for instance, will be more vigorous and prolific than potatoes that were raised Idaho in the first place. This northern vigour has been documented in strawberries and garlic as well as in spuds. The Saskatchewan Seed Potato Growers Association is so confident in the marketability of northern vigour, it has adopted the term as a registered trademark. And they have every right to be proud of their spuds. The potato is the only vegetable grown in Saskatchewan in sufficient quantities to meet local demand. In other words, we are, on the whole, potato self-sufficient.

No one knows quite why northern vigour exists, but since it is human nature to explain the unexplainable, theories abound. It could be the long dog days of a northern summer – all those many hours of sunshine in northern latitudes when the sun rises before the rooster and sets well after the kids have gone to bed. Or it might be the combination of hot days and cool nights. Perhaps the cold winters kill off any lingering diseases or pests that might slow a plant down. Or maybe they're so hardy in their northern climate that they positively flourish in the balmy breezes of the south. It could be a combination of factors, or it could be none of the above. No one knows for sure, but I sleep easier knowing that keener minds than mine are working to solve this mystery of nature. The question that most intrigues me isn't the *why* of northern vigour, but this: If I eat more spuds, will a little bit of that northern vigour rub off on me?

GROWING UP, my bedroom window overlooked the potato patch. This was my father's domain. (Mom's garden on the other side of the house grew just about everything *but* potatoes.) Every year, Dad planted several hundred hills of spuds which kept us in mashed, baked and french fried right through to spring. At which time we would cut the wizened old potatoes in half or quarters and plant them again, with Dad spading the earth while we children took turns dropping a wedge of spud into the hole in the ground. In early summer we weeded, and in midsummer we dusted for potato bugs. In fall, we dug the potatoes and washed them with a high-pressure water hose before carrying them by the bucketful into cold storage in the basement. Then, from January to April, we took turns in the cold room plucking the sprouts. Even in the dark and cold of winter, a potato wants to get going again.

My dad still tends his potato patch, growing a red-skinned variety, golden fingerlings and a Russian blue. As a family, we are potato self-sufficient.

At this point in the story, however, I feel I must fess up: I was never a great fan of potatoes. It's not that I *dislike* them, but for most of my life I've been blissfully neutral when it comes to the spud. Take 'em or leave 'em, love 'em or lump 'em, out of sight out of mind. What had once suffered for its novelty now suffered for its sheer ordinariness. I could live without 'em. Sure, for the sake of my husband, I would gladly roast potatoes with chicken or drop them into a stew, and I do love scalloped or baked, if plunked down in front of me. I am no potato snob, but left to my own culinary devices, the potato mattered not.

So, there I was at my plot in the neighbourhood community garden picking potato bugs (the community garden is organic and insecticides are not allowed, so potato bugs must be removed by hand) when I struck up a conversation with a passerby. She was visibly pregnant and had a toddler sleeping in a stroller. It is not usual to find strangers wandering in the community garden. The mere sight of it – all those luscious vegetables, the cute little garden shed, the mosaic stepping stones and rampant sunflowers – is a magnet for anyone who ever romanticized a garden. I also wished to nip in the bud an unfortunate rumour that the garden was free for the picking. A fellow gardener had already lost his prized peppers. I did not wish to arrive one day and find my potatoes had been "requisitioned" overnight.

(If you think it a contradiction that I would grow potatoes that I don't particularly care to cook, you are not thinking like a cagey peasant. I grow them because I can. Because I like digging in the dirt. Because it reminds me of spring on the farm. Because it's a family tradition. Because you never know when a famine might hit or an army might requisition every morsel in sight but the potatoes in the ground. Besides, these were my favourite potatoes, a variety called fingerlings. A fingerling potato is bent and yellow like a gnarly old thumb. No doubt a seventeenth-century doctor would take one look at it and declare it the cause of hangnails and tennis elbow.)

By now, I had collected quite a few potato bugs into a small cup. They were crawling over one another in a struggle to stay on top. Under normal circumstances, I would spill the contents onto the gravel and squish them with my boot. But this young woman seemed so charmed by the garden that I felt it best not to subject her and her unborn to the whole gooey mess.

"What are you growing?" she asked. Fair question. Just because I can identify a potato plant at twenty-five paces doesn't mean everyone can.

"Potatoes," I said.

She nodded with interest. "And where do you get the potatoes?"

"A friend gave them to me," I said. The seed stock had been provided by my friend Ramesh, who grew them on his farm.

"But," she said looking at the lush, flowering plants, "where do you *get* the potatoes?"

I looked from her to my potatoes to the rest of the garden so obviously teeming with vegetables, and back to the potato plants.

"They grow underground," I said. "You dig them up in the fall."

"Really," she said. "That's cool."

(And now if you'd like to see something really cool, I'm going to dispatch these potato bugs...)

"Look," she said, wandering in the opposite direction, "what's that?"

"A zucchini," I said. "A very overgrown zucchini."

She strolled on. Poor potato. How much ground you've gained, and lost, in five hundred years. How many people sit down every day to a plate of potatoes with nary a clue from whence you came? Do you grow on trees like apples or on vines like squash? Are you imported from Chile or China? Are you fattening? Do you cure warts? What do mashed and french fried have in common, other than serving as a worthy conduit for gravy? Clearly the potato could use a boost, a vote of confidence, a vocal champion.

As I dug those spuds, I resolved to give the potato its due. From its humble story, I had learned such valuable lessons as "don't judge a potato by its cover" and "a potato saved (and planted) is six or eight potatoes earned" and, of course, "practice makes perfect mashed potatoes." But the most important lesson I had learned from the potato was its stoic and uncompromising persistence, its tenacity in the face of hardship, its unwavering pluck. As winter settled in, I resolved to emulate the wise old tuber. Hang tight, put my best face forward, embrace the season and wait patiently for brighter days. To seal the deal, I declared my New Year's resolution: to eat more spuds.

On New Year's Eve, I prepared a celebratory dinner for which every course included a spud or two. We began with latkes and potato pakoras, then roast chicken with tartiflette (a lovely Alpine concoction of potatoes, bacon and cheese) and a fingerling and red pepper Spanish omelette, all wrapped up with mashed potato chocolate chip cookies and a hearty toast with homemade blue potato vodka. I went to bed in the wee hours confident this was one New Year's resolution that would stick, at least to my ribs.

The next day was dastardly cold. It dawned in an ice fog which cleared to a dazzling frigid afternoon, the sun amplified a thousand times (in wattage, not thermal units) off the gleaming white snow. We turned up the heat *and* lit a fire. John plugged in the car and a few hours later the engine turned somewhat reluctantly. Beyond a doubt, it was a day for curling up with a quilt, but we had been invited to the country for an outdoor game of shinny and a wiener roast. I faced the day with forbearance and bundled up: Qiviut scarf (hand-knit from the winter hair of a local herd of muskox, warm to -50); fox fur hat with ear flaps (a gift from Poland); moose hide gauntlets lined with sheep's wool (from Robertson's Trading Post in La Ronge); wool sweater (hand-knit in Nepal); two pairs of socks; lip balm; sunglasses.

If I had been listening to my inner couch potato, I would have sat by the fire and watched old movies all afternoon. But I had embraced the potato, not the palm tree, as the antidote to my winter discontent. So while every fibre of the couch in me screamed, "Are you crazy?" my inner potato gently cooed, "You'll be all right, my dear. All you need is dressing up."

## COOKING UP A MESS

MY HUSBAND HAS THE BAD HABIT of telling people I am a great cook. To set the record straight, I am not a great cook. I like to cook, and occasionally, I make something that tastes great.

I have had my share of kitchen disasters, and more often than not, there was a good cook in the room. For instance, my friend Rémi. Rémi

Cousyn, with his wife Janis, is the owner of two eateries, Calories and Souleio, and was one of the first chefs in Saskatoon to fill his menu with Saskatchewan food, well before the local movement took hold. He is an inspiration. Perhaps it took an outsider (he's from France) to see what great ingredients we have so close to home.

Cooking for a chef might be intimidating, but not with Rémi. He is always gracious in the face of good food and bad. Take, for instance, the time I smoked everyone out of the house at -30°C when the cheese bubbled over the lasagne. Or the time I added a last-minute touch of cinnamon to a lentil soup and my hand slipped. Voila, dessert! I've barely lived down the time I served bread made without the salt (terribly bland) or a cherry clafoutis *with* the pits (terribly dangerous).

There is good reason why my kitchen disasters are often witnessed by others: great cooks can multi-task a six-course meal for eight like a piece of cake, while my multi-tasking skills deteriorate long before dessert. Invariably, I bite off more than I can chew. Which explains why my greatest kitchen successes have been while cooking for just us two.

## BLUE POTATO PAKORAS

Don't try to get a jump on dinner by making the pakora batter ahead of time; by the time you cook it, the baking soda will be flat and so will your pakoras. This is basic kitchen science I learned the hard way – in front of guests, of course.

| | |
|---|---|
| ½ cup | chickpea flour (besan) |
| ¼ tsp | baking soda |

| 5 tbsp | cold water |
| ¼ cup | grated onion |
| 1 cup | grated blue potato, peeled |
| 2 tbsp | finely chopped cilantro |
| ¼ tsp | ground cumin |
| 1 | hot chili (fresh or dried), finely chopped |
| 1 tsp | salt |
| | Canola oil for frying |

Whisk the chickpea flour, baking soda and water to make a batter with the consistency of pancake batter. Stir in all the remaining ingredients except the oil.

Pour the oil into a saucepan to a depth of one inch. Heat on medium until a baking thermometer reaches 350°F. If you don't have a baking thermometer, it's ready when the surface of the oil shimmers and a drop of batter sizzles and browns.

Scoop up a soup spoon of batter and slip it into the hot oil. When the pakora is nicely golden, flip and cook the other side. This should take 5–6 minutes. (If the pakoras brown too quickly, there is a danger the batter at the centre will be uncooked. Adjust the heat if necessary.) Fry several pakoras at once but don't crowd them in the pot. Remove cooked pakoras to drain on a paper towel. Serve warm with your favourite chutney.

*This recipe is adapted from my 1969 version of *Time-Life Foods of the World: the Cooking of India.*

# JOHN'S RÖSTI

When John makes breakfast on a frigid winter morning, it's a choice of porridge or potatoes. This morning it's potatoes.

> A few leftover boiled potatoes
> A couple of green onions, chopped
> Salt and pepper
> Canola or olive oil
> A small bit of grated cheese

Peel and grate the potatoes. Mix them with the green onions and season with salt and pepper.

Pour a thin sheen of oil into a heavy frying pan and bring to medium-high heat. Scoop the potatoes into the pan, pressing them into a flat circle. Fry until the bottom is brown and crisp, then flip the potatoes over and fry the other side. (Don't expect to flip the whole thing at once like a pancake; it will fall apart. Just press it back into place.)

When the rösti is nice and brown on both sides, sprinkle the top with grated cheese. Cover and turn off the heat. Serve when the cheese is melted.

## PUMPKIN GNOCCHI WITH SAGE BUTTER SAUCE

Traditionally, gnocchi (*nyo-key*) are made with potato. Which is good. But I like them better made with pumpkin.

| | |
|---|---|
| 3 cups | puréed pumpkin |
| 1 | egg, lightly beaten |

| 3 cups | flour |
|--------|-------|
| ¼ tsp | cinnamon |
| 1 tsp | salt |
| | Several grinds of pepper |
| 2 tbsp | butter |
| 2 tbsp | olive oil |
| 1 | clove garlic, peeled |
| | About 10 fresh sage leaves |
| | Parmesan cheese for serving |

If you're starting with a real pumpkin, as opposed to canned, cut it into quarters, scrape out the seeds and bake it until soft. Cool. Scoop out the pumpkin and mash very well.

In a bowl, mix the pumpkin and egg. Stir in the flour, cinnamon, salt and pepper. Knead briefly on the counter to incorporate the flour and make a smooth sticky dough. Wrap in plastic and refrigerate for an hour.

Bring a pot of salted water to a rolling boil. Using a teaspoon, scoop up a ball of dough, roll it off the teaspoon with your fingers and drop it into the boiling water. If the dough is sticky, dip the teaspoon in cold water between each scoop. When the gnocchi float to the surface, scoop them out of the boiling water with a slotted spoon to a serving bowl. There will be too much dough to cook all at once, so do the gnocchi in batches.

Meanwhile, in a saucepan, heat the butter with the oil and garlic. Chop the sage into slivers and add to the butter. When the first batch of gnocchi is in the bowl, remove the garlic and pour the butter over the gnocchi, stirring lightly to coat. Keep them warm in a low oven as you finish cooking the gnocchi and adding them to the bowl. Serve warm sprinkled with a dash of black pepper and parmesan cheese.

# 12

# A FORK IN THE ROAD

## THE DILEMMA OVER DINNER

IT'S GETTING MORE and more difficult to invite friends for dinner. Case in point: We invited two friends to dine who gladly accepted, with a caveat. He's a no-fish vegetarian and she was "cleansing" on a diet that is gluten and lactose free. Add that up and it means no meat, fish, flour or dairy. That takes a pretty big chunk out of my culinary repertoire. No cheese plate or cold cuts. No focaccia or baguette. No pasta primavera or salt-crusted trout. No apple tart with no crème fraîche, and no whipped cream on no strawberry shortcake.

I rose to the challenge. Thanks to a menu of lentil soup, crudité with hummus (that's raw vegetables with chickpea dip) and baked meringue with fresh berries, no one went home hungry. But it proves my point – special diets are no longer the exception but the norm. Shrimp is risky, nuts are verboten, tomatoes cause acid reflux and everything from asparagus to zucchini can wreak havoc in the wrong digestive tract. Even wheat, the staff of life, is the stuff of dietary woe. No dinner invitation is complete without the corresponding question-naire: Is there anything you can't eat, won't eat, shouldn't eat or, while we're at it, reminds you of that horrible homesick week at summer camp when you were twelve?

Believe me, I am not complaining. There is much to be admired in those who exercise such discipline over the everyday pleasure of eating, whether by medical or moral prescription. I believe a consci-entious hostess should strive to satisfy the culinary requirements of all her guests. Especially, I might add, when that hostess has subjected herself to a culinary regimen of her own creation. My husband and I had embraced the "Saskatchewan diet" with the fervour of a lactose-intolerant vegetarian allergic to seafood *and* nuts. And while we did not foist our special diet on our dinner hosts, we did take great delight in imposing it on our unsuspecting dinner guests. A morsel of moral conviction never hurt anyone.

Of course, it didn't take long for the naysayers to come out of the kitchen. With headlines like "Local Schmocal" and "Extreme Eating," they bit into the local food movement with the zeal of a dog gnawing a fresh bone. Which is not a bad thing. The naysayers point out quite correctly that locally produced food is not necessarily healthier, greener or holier-than-hotcakes. It can be just as impersonal and unsustainable as industrial food produced anywhere in the world. Local farmers aren't any *less* likely to use fossil fuels or treat their livestock inhumanely or misuse the environment. There's no guarantee that locally processed foods won't make you sick or be the subject of a food recall. Pathogens know no borders.

The critics also correctly point out that counting miles is not quite as simple as counting calories. The road less travelled is not always paved with a smaller environmental footprint because it doesn't take into account *how* the food was produced. Was it raised on grass or grain? Was it cultivated with tractors or hoes? Is it organic or sprayed? Irrigated or pelted with rain? Grown under lights or sunshine? Shipped by truck or ocean freighter? Stored or picked fresh? Natural and raw or processed and packaged in plastic? The factors that influence the environmental impact are not quite as straightforward as a prairie grid road.

Take, for instance, a study by the Leopold Centre for Sustainable Agriculture in Ames, Iowa, which calculated the environmental impact of table grapes arriving at Philadelphia, the number one US port for imported fruits and vegetables. The study found that grapes shipped from Chile require no more fuel than grapes arriving by truck from California, despite the fact that Chile is much further away. This, we learn, is because ocean freighters offer economies of scale: with so many goods on board, every item shares just a fraction of the fuel expenditure.

Then there was the news from New Zealand: lamb from Down Under has a smaller environmental footprint than English lamb, even after factoring in the transportation to a grocery store within sight of Buckingham Palace and Big Ben. The difference is in the way it's raised. In New Zealand, lambs graze on grassy pastures, while in England, where pastures are smaller and less productive, lambs rely on cultivated feed. Grain is a gas guzzler. Grass grows on sunshine.

Then there was the flap in England over green beans from Kenya. It seemed an outright scandal to import green beans from Kenya when they grow so close to home, until it was pointed out that these hand-grown green beans from Africa had a smaller environmental footprint than green beans farmed the modern way in England, even with the airfare factored in. In other words, Kenya's green beans might be a better choice if the environment is your main concern. When the measure is greenhouse gas emissions, farmers with hoes and oxen will always outperform farmers with tractors and petro-chemical sprays.

Counting miles can be just as futile when it comes to processed foods. Take that can of chickpeas, for instance. The chickpeas may be local to Saskatchewan but, chances are, the processing is not. It's a one-way trip to the factory "out east" and a round trip back to a grocery store in Swift Current or Saskatoon. In this scenario, a can of Saskatchewan chickpeas has a smaller environmental footprint in Montreal than in Maple Creek, closer to the factory than the field where it was grown. Imagine the supermarket flyer advertising that deal: Two-for-one special. Double your miles with every bite. All the flavour and twice the guilt.

The fact is, eating is one of the least environmentally friendly things we do. The global food system is positively hooked on fossil fuels at every stage, from tractor fuel to synthetic fertilizers and pesticides (which are derived from fossil fuels), to factories and refrigerated trucks. Consider this statistic, gleaned from the writing of activist author Michael Pollan: In 1940, one calorie of fossil fuel energy was used to produce about two calories of food. Today, it is the exact opposite and worse: ten calories of fossil fuel energy produce just one calorie of food. And here's the rub: transportation is a small piece of the pie – about 11 percent, according to a study from the Carnegie Mellon

University in Pittsburg, which determined that by far the biggest chunk of greenhouse gases, more than 80 percent, is related to the production of food. In other words, what happens on the farm.

Take, for instance, that juicy all-beef hamburger patty. It could be one of the most environmentally unfriendly foods of all. The authors of the Carnegie Mellon study found that the worldwide production of red meat creates three times more greenhouse gases than chicken or fish; dairy produces twice as much. All told, they say, the impact of red meat equals chicken, fish, grains, fruits and vegetables combined. This led the researchers to the bold conclusion that we would do better, in terms of greenhouse gas emissions, to skip red meat and dairy one day a week than to eat local for the other six. If the environment is your main concern, vegans have it over locavores any day of the week.

Of course, there are exceptions to this rule, and one of them is sitting here on my dinner plate: a juicy, extra-lean, grass-fed, all-natural ground beef hamburger patty from a Texas Longhorn raised by a friend-of-a-friend named Ruth. This is not the ground beef populating the grocery stores, but it is available to the discerning eater who doesn't mind shopping off the beaten path. Down in my freezer you'll find grass-fed lamb, not from New Zealand, but from the Richardson sisters' farm just up the road at Langham. And here is a jar of pickled green beans, not from Africa, but from the backyard garden of my friend Joanne, who lives on the next block. As for table grapes, I tend not to buy them, except in the form of table wine.

I am reminded of something I read by Wendell Berry, the farmer-philosopher from rural Kentucky, who wrote that "eating is an agricultural act." What could be more simple yet more profound? If we eat, we are *ipso facto* part of the agricultural process. And if we are part of the agricultural process, we have an opportunity – Wendell might say a responsibility – to be curious enough to ask questions and to make some tough choices about the food we consume. As Wendell puts it: "How we eat determines how the world is used."

I am also reminded of those sage words attributed to Yogi Berra, the Baseball Hall of Famer with a unique way of putting things: "When you come to the fork in the road, take it." In other words, when faced with options, you've got no choice but to make a choice. For better or worse, day in and day out, one step forward and no steps back. When I came to that fork in the road, staring to my left down the well-worn byway of modern industrial food systems and, to my right, down the prairie trail of local food ways, I chose the path less travelled. To be sure, it's a slower route, with more twists and turns and fewer billboards vying for my attention, but it's a scenic road and I like the folks I meet along on the way. I feel at home there. So, while I respect the vegans for their convictions, I am not about to give up on cheeseburgers just yet.

TOWARD THE MIDDLE OF APRIL, we found ourselves in a quandary over eggs. This quandary was not, as you might think, related to the dire warning that eggs (with 215 milligrams of cholesterol) are bad for the health. I never paid much attention to those warnings, and a good thing, too, since the fear-mongers have recently reversed their position and announced that eggs are really good for you. As part of a well-rounded, five-vegetables-a-day, lean-as-caffeine (which is also good or bad for you, depending on the headlines), wholesome and balanced diet, a couple of eggs won't kill you.

Funny, isn't it, how we could be warned off a natural food like eggs for all those years while encouraged to eat something so completely unnatural as trans fat in our margarine. What's next? Will we hear that an apple a day is one too many, and that butylated hydroxyanisole is good for the heart? No doubt, a short time later, the apple will be reha-bilitated and butylated hydroxyanisole, a common food preservative, will be vilified for causing cancer in rats. Since I married a fellow from the Dairy State (heard to utter "lips that touch margarine will never touch mine"), we eat butter with our toast and eggs. Perhaps that leaves room for a little butylated hydroxyanisole every now and then. All in moderation, I say. Unless, of course, you're on the egg diet.

The egg diet is born out of necessity: necessity to clean up the last batch of eggs before the next batch arrives. Since I had become an egg lady, brokering dozens of free-range farm eggs from my refrigerator door, we had grown accustomed to eating eggs whenever the fancy struck. It might be scrambled for breakfast, or egg salad sandwiches for lunch, or spaghetti carbonara for supper (a yummy mixture of bacon, eggs and pasta). Invited to a potluck, I would choose between a vegetable frittata and devilled eggs. On special occasions, when dessert was in order, I could whip up a sponge cake or a baked meringue. Eggs were the handy, cheap, fast, versatile, delicious, nutritious and, given their unnatural abundance in our refrigerator, the natural choice when the cupboard was otherwise bare.

Every now and then, however, despite my best efforts to devour and disseminate twenty dozen eggs, Al would announce his intention to come to town with another twenty dozen before the last batch of eggs had fully disappeared. That's when the egg diet came in handy. In order to clean out the old and make room for the new, we adopted a rigorous regimen of eggs three meals a day. Scrambled for breakfast, *and* egg salad sandwiches for lunch, *and* spaghetti carbonara for supper. Devilled, baked, whipped and souffléd. Whoever said you have to crack an egg to make an omelette got it wrong; you have to crack three or four. The more the better. We never tired of eggs. And we never ran out. Except on those very rare occasions, and this was one of them, when I brokered so many eggs I had shortchanged myself. The fridge was glaringly, shockingly empty of eggs.

This was the source of my dilemma. John's birthday was close upon us and I could not let the day pass without a cake. And a cake needs eggs. I could do what millions of home cooks do every day: write "eggs" on my grocery list, then go to the supermarket and buy some. A simple plan but fraught with complexities. I had grown so accustomed to my robust country eggs, with their thick brownish shells and big orangey yolks, that I had developed a strong, perhaps unhealthy, prejudice against the pale, dainty, uniform eggs for sale in the grocery store. But it was more than appearances. These were the eggs of my childhood, a reminder of a time when I slipped into the dim henhouse, gathered the warm eggs into a paint pail, wiped them with a damp cloth and lined them up in mismatched recycled cartons so my mom could sell them in town. If salt makes food takes better, nostalgia makes it taste great.

Besides, I knew exactly where Al's eggs came from. I knew nothing about the eggs in the store. Would they be locally laid? Did the hens have an opportunity to wander outside and peck about the yard? Did they eat grass and bugs (the source of those yellow yolks)? It has come to light that diet makes a difference (if it's true that you are what you eat, wouldn't it hold for chickens, too?): "outdoor" eggs have more vitamin D, E, beta carotene and omega-3 than "indoor" eggs, and less cholesterol, too. Would I compromise more than my principles by heading to the store?

I came to that fork in the road and turned left. And that's how I found myself, grocery list in hand, staring into a cool, gleaming wall of supermarket eggs. Things had changed since I had been here last. What had once been a relatively minor decision (small, medium, large or xl) had grown into a major compendium of egg options. White or brown (though not in the same carton), free-run, free-range, cage-free, organic, omega-3, vegetarian, vitamin-enhanced, liquid and even yolk-free pre-scrambled eggs. No doubt, these "new and improved" varieties would amaze that venerable old egg, Humpty, while meeting the dietary needs of all the king's men. I was half surprised not to find a new generation of hard-boiled, yolk-reduced, salt-and-pepper-flavoured, already-coloured-for-Easter eggs. Now wouldn't that take the fun out of everything?

With so many choices, it should be easy to find a designer egg with near the same properties as Al's farm eggs, but, I quickly discovered, not at Al's price. Designer eggs are considerably more expensive. A bit shocking really, when you are unaccustomed to reading price tags. I suppose this can be expected, given the level of scientific research necessary to create an "indoor" omega-3 egg, not to mention the specially formulated chicken feed, plus any bonus add-ons such as organic or free range. It all adds up, unless you're farming like Al, in which case, it all adds down. I suppose the recycled egg cartons save a few cents, too.

I'm not much for budgets, so I can't say with certainty if it costs more or less to eat locally. It certainly costs less if you avoid the higher priced imports such as shrimp and avocados, and pass up expensive processed and convenience foods. I save money by buying in bulk, but pay more if it is certified organic. I save money by picking berries and other fruit, but if time is money, spend considerably more by canning and freezing it myself. I save money by skipping the middle agent, but spend money when I drive any distance to acquire the goods. When all is said and done, John and I probably spend about the same for food as we did before we ventured into the local food basket, but we are getting more for our money. As far as I'm concerned, fresh, wholesome, naturally produced and tastier food is worth a buck or two.

The truth is, I pay what the farmers ask, confident they are charging no more, or less, than a living wage. I like a bargain as much as the next person, but when I have an opportunity to buy, say, mushrooms picked just yesterday, I don't ask how much but how many. If my primary goal is to support and celebrate Saskatchewan agriculture, and my secondary goal is to do something good for the environment, and my third goal is to eat well and have fun while I'm at it, then it stands to reason that saving pennies is farther down my list. This is not to say I am extravagant – far from it. I'm not a fancy cook; my tastes run more with the king's men than with the king. I'd rather cook a hardy chicken cacciatore than a veal cordon bleu, and six-course dinners are only pleasant when they emerge from someone else's kitchen. I made a choice to put my money where my mouth is, and found it not a high price to pay.

As for those eggs – I bought them, a plain old carton of plain white large. And no one eating that birthday cake noticed the difference.

On the 366th day of our local diet, which is to say, the first day of no diet at all, I went to the grocery store without a list. I pushed my cart aimlessly through the aisles, liberated from rules and caveats, unfettered by labels and points of origin, free to pluck absolutely anything from the freezers or off the shelf. What's for dinner? Anything at all. A thousand options or more, all clamouring for my attention with catchy labels and enticing declarations of healthy virtues and nutritional aids, more of this and less of that, 30-percent larger and 50-cents off. The floodgates were open and the noise was deafening. Didn't I have some pork chops in the freezer? Wasn't there a jar of pears in the cupboard and the makings of coleslaw in the fridge? I grabbed a jar of peanut butter, a few bananas and a package of John's favourite store-bought cookies which he had forsaken (as far as I knew) for one whole year. It felt good to be a citizen of the world, but all I wanted was to eat at home.

TWO YEARS ON, John and I sat down to a local dinner, Czech style. We ate in honour of our neighbour, Rosie, and her husband, Albert, both of whom were ethnic Czech. Albert had passed away long before we occupied our house, and Rosie had recently followed him to the great beyond. On the following day, their little white house with red trim had a date with the wrecking ball. Our year of eating locally was well behind us, but we had a new project to occupy our waking hours: we were building a house.

This was not just any house. It would be a post-and-beam house, built with big timbers joined by mortise and tenon, and pinned together with wooden pegs, like the sturdy old houses and barns that have stood for hundreds of years in the Old County. In keeping with our local sentiments, it would be constructed with timbers hewn from the spruce forest of northern Saskatchewan and dimensioned at the Mennonite sawmill outside the town of Rosthern. John had already built several garage-sized timber frames in Saskatoon (and a barn in the countryside) but this would be, so we were informed at City Hall, the first timber-frame house within the city limits.

The basic design was simple. An open living-dining-kitchen area on the main floor; bedrooms-office-bath on the second. A staircase deftly positioned between the beams so as not to bump your head on the way up. Big exposed timbers overhead. John had sketched the house on scrap paper and our friend David had transformed it into a proper architectural design. It was shaping up nicely.

As for me, I had been politely but firmly informed that my input was quite unnecessary except in the realm of the kitchen. I did not find this to be a serious affront. For years I had been nagging John to renovate my kitchen and now, instead of a new kitchen, I was getting a whole new house. Who could complain about that? It was sure proof that if a little nagging doesn't work, a lot of nagging can net big results.

"Can I have a bread-kneading table with a granite top?" I asked over dinner.

"I guess so," said John.

"And a flour bin?"

"OK."

"And a shelf for my collection of vintage *Time-Life Foods of the World* cookbooks?"

"Sure."

"And a rack to display my collection of coffee mugs from cities around the world?" There was no response, so I added for good measure, "And my collection of tacky tourist spoons to match?"

Still nothing. Silence is golden. I was on a roll.

"And my collection of chickens?" (My friend Janis and I exchange gifts of a chicken motif, such as chicken egg cups, chicken napkins and chicken salt and pepper shakers.) "And my collection of vintage Depression glass?"

John gave me a reproving look. "Is it a kitchen or a museum?"

"Obviously," I said, "it's my *kitch*-in."

When my thoughts turned to Rosie, I remembered her knocking on our back door with a plate of fresh-from-the-oven gingersnaps or a couple of red tomatoes from her garden, which always seemed to ripen sooner than mine. I remembered our wedding day when she sat beside me like an honoured grandmother (our own grandmothers being there in spirit only) and gave us her prescription for a happy marriage, in writing, should we chance to forget. Sage advice, like "never lie to each other" and "never go to bed angry." The way she talked, hers had been a union made in heaven. Albert was a carpenter of the old school, trained behind the Iron Curtain, and we thought he might approve of our new house.

The year after our wedding, John and I took a rambling trip to Europe and Africa with an itinerary loosely based on serendipity and the generosity of friends and strangers we met along the way. We house-sat in Senegal, lived in a Tuscan village, visited an old college pal in Vienna, looked up a friend who was teaching English in Poland and hung out in Wimbledon in the tennis off-season. In between, we made a small detour en route through the Czech Republic to a little village with an unpronounceable name, which we wrote on a piece of paper to show the driver of the bus: Zdebořice. It was Albert's hometown.

The bus dropped us at the side of the highway beside a small farm with laundry flapping on the line and a big rooster lording over his flock within a stone fence. Our destination was perched on top of a hill behind the farm, straight up as the crow flies. We crossed the highway and walked up the lane. The lady of the house saw us coming and hurried out to meet us, wiping her hands on her ample apron. It was our intention to ask permission to leave our backpacks in her yard while we walked up the hill to Zdebořice and back, but she would have none of it. We were invited in for a bowl of chicken soup, after which her husband would drive us up the hill and introduce us to someone who might remember Albert Houdek.

To make a long story short, we went up the hill in a dusty Lada, met the mayor, toured the village, took a picture of Albert's boyhood home, slapped back a few hospitable shots of bekarovka in the mayor's house and came back down the hill, coasting in the old Lada to save a bit of gas. Then we sat down at the kitchen table next to a massive masonry stove for a cup of coffee and a piece of cherry cake. For the life of me, I can't remember how we conducted these conversations because they spoke no English and we spoke no Czech. I suppose it was the international language of hospitality and the universal impulse to sit down together over something good to eat and drink.

"Don't look down," said John with false frivolity in his voice, "but the cake is full of ants."

"Really?" I said, trying *very* hard not to look down.

"Don't stop eating," he said, taking a bite and washing it down with swig of coffee. "I don't want to insult them, they've been so nice to us."

I smiled and swallowed hard, nodding in agreement, then glanced nonchalantly at my plate. Two big black ants scurried over top and disappeared into an air pocket created by the cherries in the cake.

"Their eyesight must be pretty bad," said John, while pointing at a photograph on the wall. The woman began an animated explanation by which we understood it to be a picture of her daughter who was teaching at a university in Prague.

With attention deflected, I took a bit of cake on my fork, a piece carefully calculated to be no bigger than the length of an ant, and gave it a good hard look. If I could see a head or tail wiggling out either side, I wouldn't eat it. But if I couldn't see an ant, well, I have probably eaten worse things without knowing it. For all I know, ants are a good source of protein. Perhaps they aid digestion. Maybe they even taste sweet. Didn't I see on TV that some cultures snack on ants? Aren't they considered a delicacy when dipped in chocolate? Or fried up with salt? I wasn't sure of the maximum residue level or acceptable parts per million of the ordinary black ant, but I was quite sure that one or two of them wouldn't kill me.

"Mmmm, good," I said, holding up the last forkful of cake at eye level. No ants. I ate it quickly. The woman offered us another piece.

"Oh, no," we both said at once. John pointed to his watch. "*Autobus.*"

We bade them farewell, hoisted our backpacks and walked out to the highway to catch the next bus. That evening, we washed down the remaining ant residue with a maximum level of excellent Czech beer.

In Italy, such humble peasant cuisine could be called *cucina povera*, a term that implies all the fresh, hearty flavours of the local countryside brought together with more TLC than GDP. *Cucina povera* may be "cooking of the poor" but there is nothing poor about the cooking. It's as rich and delicious as money *can't* buy. A cuisine that personifies that old Roman saying, "The more you spend, the worse you eat."

And now, our new house had given us a whole new reason to eat like peasants. John was investing his sweat equity and I was earning an income for two. In other words, we were spending like drunken sailors whose paycheques had just been cut in half. This diminished state of affairs required a willingness to curb excesses and a fair bit of economizing in the kitchen. If it's true that the more you spend the worse you eat, we were going to eat very, very well.

On the eve of the demolition, we walked one last time through the empty rooms of Rosie's house, remembering our dear sweet white-haired friend, then came home to our Czech dinner Saskatchewan-style: pork goulash with anise seed, braised cabbage and bacon, buttered egg noodles, dark rye bread and for dessert, a cherry cake, all washed down with cold mugs of Czech pilsner. I was already pining for the first dinner party in my new house.

"You can have plenty of dinner parties," said John, "but remember they have to be cheap."

"Not just cheap," I said. "*Povera.*"

---

## THE LOCAL PARADOX

PERHAPS IT SEEMS IRONIC to promote a local diet in a place like Saskatchewan that relies so heavily on the export of food. Our farmers are so prolific, they'd be lost without their international markets. With a population just above the million mark, there aren't near enough people in Saskatchewan to eat everything they produce. We locavores make a very small dent in the big scheme of things.

But it's a significant dent for those farmers who care about us. Feeding the local population should be a viable option, supported by agricultural ministries and local grocery stores, available to consumers without much fuss and bother. In other words, a natural complement to a proficient and prolific industrial food system. What seems more ironic, in my view, is that so few us who live here eat the bounty of a land as fertile as Saskatchewan. Wouldn't it be nice if that were an easy choice?

# NICE SALAD

The French have the Salade Nicoise, named for the city of Nice. (The salad *neece-swaz* from the city of *neece*.) There, they make it with tuna, but since tuna is not a Saskatchewan fish, I make it with whitefish or trout. Either way, it's very nice.

|  | Several small potatoes, boiled and cubed |
|---|---|
| ½ | small onion, thinly sliced |
| ½ | green pepper, thinly sliced |
| 10–12 | green beans, cooked and chopped |
|  | Small handful of fresh basil, thinly sliced |
| 2–4 | tomatoes, cut in wedges |
| 2–4 | hardboiled eggs, cut in wedges |
| 1 cup | cooked trout, flaked |

DRESSING

|  | Juice of one-half juicy lemon |
|---|---|
|  | An equal amount of olive oil |
| ½ tsp | Dijon mustard |
|  | Dash of salt and pepper |

Make the dressing by whisking the lemon juice, mustard, salt and pepper. Drizzle in the olive oil, whisking all the while to form a creamy dressing.

In a bowl, gather together the potatoes, onion, green pepper and green beans. Toss in the dressing. Marinate a few minutes or a few hours. At the last moment, mix in the basil.

To serve, place the potato mixture onto a platter. Place the wedges of tomato and hardboiled egg around the edge of the salad. Mound the fish in the centre. Drizzle the eggs, tomato and fish with olive oil and a sprinkle of salt and pepper. This is a pretty salad, so make sure everyone admires it before digging in.

---

# KIBBE NAYYA

My girlfriend Paula is a fabulous cook. Let her loose in the kitchen with a lemon and a sprig of mint and she can make a Lebanese feast. In her family, Kibbe Nayya is made the same day the lamb is slaughtered. The paradox is that Paula doesn't eat red meat, but she sure can "cook" it!

| | |
|---|---|
| 1 | shoulder of lamb (about 2 lbs/1 kg of meat) |
| 4 | green onions |
| | Handful *each* of fresh mint and basil |
| 2 tsp | *each* salt and pepper |
| 1 tsp | cayenne |
| ½ tsp | *each* mace, cinnamon and cumin |
| 1 cup | cracked wheat (called "burghul" in Lebanon) |
| | Olive oil for drizzling |
| | Lots of thin green onions and extra mint leaves |
| | Pita bread |

Put the lamb (minus the bone), onions, mint and basil through a meat grinder. Mix in the spices.

Cover the cracked wheat with hot water and let stand ten minutes, until softened (or follow package instructions). Drain well. Mix the cracked wheat into the meat mixture and knead as you would bread dough, adding a drop of water from time to time, until the mixture is silky smooth.

Taste and add more spices to suit your palate. Paula says salt and pepper are the most important spices; the others should be evident but subdued.

Spread the lamb mixture into a flat serving bowl. Using a finger, run three furrows the length of the lamb. Drizzle a generous amount of olive oil into the furrows. Garnish the edges of the bowl with thin green onions and fresh mint leaves. To eat, scoop the Kibbe Nayya with a chunk of pita bread, top it with a green onion and a mint leaf and pop it into your mouth.

---

# CURRIED PEAR AND SQUASH SOUP

This year, my New Year's resolution is to eat more homemade soup. And what could be more *cucina povera* than that? This soup was Week One.

| | |
|---|---|
| 1 | medium butternut or acorn squash |
| 2 tbsp | butter |
| 1 | large onion, thinly sliced |
| 1–2 tbsp | curry powder |
| | Salt and white pepper |
| 4 cups | water |
| 1 cup | canned pears, chopped, and their juice (about ½ cup juice) |
| ½ cup | cream |
| 1 cup | cooked wild rice |

Unless you have leftovers, cook the wild rice first because it takes a while. To cook wild rice, boil it in plenty of water with a pinch of salt for about an hour. Some people like wild rice a bit chewy while others like it cooked so soft it pops. Bite into a grain to make sure it's cooked the way you like it.

Peel, seed and chop the squash into small chunks. You should have 4–5 cups of squash.

Melt the butter in a soup pot and sauté the onion. After a few minutes, stir in 1 tbsp curry powder, salt and pepper. Cook until the onions are soft. Add the water and the squash. Bring to a boil, turn down the heat and simmer. Add the chopped pears and their juice. Cook another 15 minutes or so.

Remove from the heat and cool. Purée the soup in a blender, returning it to a clean pot. Reheat. Taste for seasoning: if you like it hot, add the rest of the curry powder. Stir in the cream but don't boil. If the soup is too thick, add a bit more water. To serve, ladle the hot soup into bowls, placing a heaping spoonful of cooked wild rice in the centre of each bowl.

## ACKNOWLEDGEMENTS

Many thanks to my husband, John Bertolini, a willing and good-humoured partner in my culinary adventures, and to my parents, Dennis and Gail Ehman, for filling my childhood memories with good, farm food. Thank you to CBC Radio producers Sean Prpick and Michelle McCaw who found my food stories worthy of air time, and to Joanne Paulson, former lifestyles editor at the Saskatoon *StarPhoenix*, for championing my food column at a time when a local diet seemed a tad unusual. Thank you to the editors of *Prairies North Magazine*, Lionel and Michelle Hughes, who recognize food as integral to the cultural fabric of our fair province. Thank you to the Saskatchewan Arts Board for the funding and vote of confidence that set this book in motion. And a big big thanks to my editor Roberta Coulter and to Coteau Books for polishing my collection of stories and producing such a beautiful, memorable book. But most of all, thank you to all the farmers, gardeners and processors whose passion for quality, flavour and local commerce made my year of eating locally so delicious and so fun that I simply could not eat any other way.

## PHOTOGRAPHY

Patricia Holdsworth Photography: cover, pages 62 and 148.

# RECIPE INDEX

**FSC**

Mixed Sources

Cert no. SW-COC-001271

© 1996 FSC

## ENVIRONMENTAL BENEFITS STATEMENT

**Coteau Books** saved the following resources by printing the pages of this book on chlorine free paper made with 10% post-consumer waste.

| TREES | WATER | SOLID WASTE | GREENHOUSE GASES |
|---|---|---|---|
| **5** | **2,111** | **128** | **438** |
| FULLY GROWN | GALLONS | POUNDS | POUNDS |

Calculations based on research by Environmental Defense and the Paper Task Force. Manufactured at Friesens Corporation

*Printed and bound in Canada by Friesens*